YOUTH, WORK AND THE POST-FORDIST SELF

David Farrugia

BRISTOL
UNIVERSITY
PRESS

First published in Great Britain in 2021 by

Bristol University Press
University of Bristol
1-9 Old Park Hill
Bristol
BS2 8BB
UK
t: +44 (0)117 954 5940
e: bup-info@bristol.ac.uk

Details of international sales and distribution partners are available at bristoluniversitypress.co.uk

© Bristol University Press 2021

British Library Cataloguing in Publication Data
A catalogue record for this book is available from the British Library

ISBN 978-1-5292-1005-7 hardcover
ISBN 978-1-5292-1008-8 ePub
ISBN 978-1-5292-1007-1 ePdf

The right of David Farrugia to be identified as author of this work has been asserted by him
in accordance with the Copyright, Designs and Patents Act 1988.

Bristol University Press works to counter discrimination on grounds of
gender, race, disability, age and sexuality.

Cover design: Blu Inc
Front cover image: Stocksy

Bristol University Press uses environmentally responsible print partners.

Printed in Great Britain by CPI Group (UK) Ltd, Croydon, CR0 4YY

Contents

About the Author

David Farrugia is Senior Lecturer in Sociology at the University of Newcastle and co-director of the Newcastle Youth Studies Network. His work focuses on youth, work, labour and globalization. He has written on rural and regional youth, young people and the service economy, and the formation of young people as post-Fordist workers. His work is published in *The British Journal of Sociology*, *The Sociological Review* and *The Journal of Youth Studies*. His previous books include *Youth Homelessness in Late Modernity: Reflexive Identities and Moral Worth* (2015) and *Spaces of Youth: Work, Citizenship and Culture in a Global Context* (2018).

Young People, Work and Society: New Terrain

This book is about the formation of young people as workers. It explores the position of youth within transformations in the relationship between work and the self that are emblematic of contemporary capitalism in the global north. In particular, the book explores the relationship between youth, work and identity by examining how notions of economic productivity form part of youth subjectivities, and therefore how young people cultivate themselves as subjects of value to the contemporary labour force. The book will show that the capacity for economic productivity has become intertwined with the ethic of self-realization characteristic of late modern subjectivities. The realization of the self through work has become critical to the way that young people imagine themselves and their prospects of happiness now and in the future. Young people are therefore at the forefront of what Kathi Weeks (2011) has called the 'post-Fordist work ethic', or the promise of personal fulfilment and self-actualization through labour that is increasingly experienced as a requirement for a fulfilling life in late capitalism. In this way, the formation of young people as workers provides an insight into the increasingly critical position that youth now occupy within the dynamics of subjectivity and economic productivity characteristic of post-Fordist societies.

With this focus, the book develops intersections between youth studies and labour studies (Tannock, 2001; Besen-Cassino, 2014), and departs from approaches to the relationship between young people and work that are currently dominant in research as well as in social policy interventions into young people's lives. Young people's relationship to the labour market is a long-standing preoccupation of academics and governmental authorities. Youth is a critical point of intervention into the labour force, with a constantly shifting array of educational, disciplinary and technical interventions all focused on turning young people into workers. However, this process – the formation of young people as workers – receives little attention and is poorly understood. Instead, as Stuart Tannock observed two decades ago (Tannock, 2001), the basic focus of existing approaches to youth and work is the role of employment in the biographical movement into adulthood, however ambiguous and complex that adulthood has become. For governmental authorities, the aim (or, more specifically, the requirement) is that young people become employed, and thereby move towards an economically productive adulthood. This takes place through the accumulation of resources (such as educational qualifications) that can be exchanged on the labour market for a wage, as well as a range of more or less punitive interventions into the lives of young people who do not make this transition. For many sociologists, the concerns are essentially the same, with an additional focus on social inequalities in employment outcomes, a critical examination of the conditions under which young people work and a more sociological focus on the causes of unemployment. In this perspective, what counts is not merely that young people are employed, but how 'lovely' or 'lousy' those jobs might be in terms of remuneration, security and working conditions (Furlong et al, 2017), as well as acknowledging the structural dimensions of unemployment.

The formation of young people as workers – that is, as subjects who must understand themselves as economically productive and who must cultivate the capacity for economic productivity as part of their identities – has to this point been a marginal concern. This is despite the fact that contemporary labour studies suggest the relationship between youth and work is transforming amid shifts in the relationship between work, consumption and identity in contemporary capitalism. Young labour has become critical to many economic sectors, and youthful attributes such as aspiration and flexibility are increasingly valorized as a quality of workers in general (Farrugia, 2018a, 2020). Young workers are also at the forefront of changes in the meaning of work, which is promoted and approached through notions of branding and personal development that resemble processes of consumption (Besen-Cassino, 2014). Classed and gendered subjectivities have also transformed as a result of deindustrialization, creating anxieties about 'redundant' masculinities (McDowell, 2003) as well as new forms of gendered subjectivity through the disciplinary requirements of service labour (Roberts, 2018). Developing this nexus of youth and labour studies, this book pursues a paradigm shift in studies of youth and work, moving away from understanding young people in terms of whether they get jobs and towards an examination of how youth itself is formed through the requirement to become a worker.

In order to achieve this shift, this book situates the formation of youth subjectivities as part of the dynamics of labour, subjectivity and value in what has been called 'post-Fordist' capitalism. While the concept of post-Fordism has had impacts in areas as diverse as political economy, geography, sociology and cultural studies (Amin, 2003), what I am particularly interested in here is the suggestion that the dynamics of post-Fordist value creation involve the production and performance of subjectivity in its most general sense as critical to working practices and the value of labour. Life itself has become a source of value, at least according to autonomist Marxists such as Hardt and Negri (2004), and this process is making the boundaries between the productive and unproductive dimensions of the self increasingly difficult to discern (Adkins and Lury, 1999). All aspects of subjectivity are now implicated in the position a worker occupies in the labour force. This is also implied by concept of the post-Fordist work ethic as theorized by Kathi Weeks (2011), which forms the basis for the conceptual framework adopted in this book. Through the post-Fordist work ethic, Weeks (2011) traces and critiques shifts in the relationship between work and the self within changes in the social organization of employment, labouring practices and valorization processes to show how the ethical requirement to commit the self to labour produces subjectivities in different periods of capitalism. The post-Fordist work ethic suggests that the contemporary self is imbricated in the requirements of work in unprecedented ways, owing to what Weeks (2011, p 75) has called the 'ontological reward' of the contemporary work ethic, which makes social existence as such contingent on a commitment to work.

While the meaning of these claims will be explored and interrogated more fully in the chapters that follow, these arguments create questions about how young people are formed as workers, and make the task of understanding how youth cultivate the capacity to produce economic value increasingly urgent. If contemporary capitalism produces value from life itself, how are young people's subjectivities enrolled into the formation of the post-Fordist labour force? How do the demands of economic productivity relate to young people's identities, and how are young people cultivating the capacities that will allow them to produce value at work? How do differently positioned young people respond to the imperative to become productive, and how does the relationship between class, identity and work shape the practices that young people draw upon to form identities as workers? These are the kinds of questions explored in this book.

To substantiate these arguments and situate the significance of these issues, the remainder of this chapter sketches out what I will suggest are some contemporary problems in studies of youth, identity, work and social class, focusing on two key concerns. First, the chapter explores the intellectual frameworks brought to bear on the relationship between youth and work, including the dominance of youth transitions as an academic and social policy concern and the more recent emergence of political economy of youth perspectives. My discussion here includes a critique of the way that young people are imagined as economic subjects in these frameworks, as well as the limited understandings of social class that these perspectives imply. Second, the chapter explores contemporary understandings of social class from the perspective of work. The chapter critiques the retreat of work from studies of class, which are increasingly focused on cultural politics, consumption practices and symbolic value. In particular, while notions of symbolic value have positioned subjectivity as critical to class relations, it has resulted in an obfuscation of work as a site for subject formation despite the historical (and necessary) focus on work, labour and value in theories of social class. The chapter concludes with an overview of the book and a discussion of the empirical research that forms the basis for Chapters 3, 4 and 5.

From youth transitions to the subjectification function of work

The relationship between youth and work is a long-standing but enormously contested intellectual and political issue. The study of young people and work provides an evocative example of the complex relationship between governmental interventions, intellectual frameworks and academic research on a topic that strikes at the heart of social and economic relations. The history of this field is connected with efforts on the part of national governments and other political actors to produce and govern a useful labour force through interventions into youth. These interventions have impacted upon the aims and assumptions made by competing intellectual and disciplinary frameworks concerning the economic situation of young people. However, while there is an extensive history of sociological work that critiques the ambitions of governmental actors, in many substantive areas social scientists have followed the problematizing logic established in governmental agendas, even if they have been critical of the individualistic assumptions that have tended to underpin these interventions. This has ignored what, following Weeks (2011), I will call the subjectification function of work, or the role of work in the production of subjectivities and social relations. In what follows, I substantiate these claims by interrogating two contemporary frameworks for studies of youth and work: the dominant youth transitions approach and the recently emerging political economy of youth approach.

Beyond youth transitions

Christine Griffin's (1993) overview of the field of school to work transitions provides an important history of the way that young people's relationship to employment emerged as a topic of intellectual and social policy concern in the post-war United Kingdom (UK) and United States (US). While it was published in the early 1990s, Griffin's discussion of the development of this area remains relevant today, especially in emphasizing what she refers to as the "one Big Question: the incidence and explanation of inequalities in the move from full-time education to waged work" (Griffin, 1993, p 28; see also Tannock, 2001, p 23). Addressing this one big question has been the main goal of research on young people's relationship with work. According to Griffin, concern with young people's biographical movements through employment began amid labour shortages occurring during the era of economic rebuilding following the Second World War. At this time, governments investigated young people's movement into work in an effort to supply labour to capital during a time of economic change, and drew primarily on individualistic psychological approaches (such as concepts of occupational choice) in order to understand how young people navigated their way into particular forms of employment. In the 1970s, the institutionalization of more critical sociological perspectives, including especially Marxist and neo-Marxist approaches, led to the emergence of structurally oriented explanations for occupational stratification. Individualistic and psychological models remained dominant at the level of social policy. Regardless of the orientation, the key concern remained young people's biographical pathways into employment. That is, the concept of youth transitions is about asking when young people get jobs, what jobs they get and how this connects with their social background.

In the 1980s and subsequently, young people's relationship with work has been framed by the implementation and contestation of neoliberal governmental agendas. Griffin's review conducted in 1993 captures the period immediately following the Thatcher and Reagan eras in the UK and US, in which an explosion in levels of youth unemployment took place alongside increasingly vitriolic rhetoric about young people's attitudes towards work and an increasingly punitive range of interventions into young people's lives designed to (at least nominally) reduce unemployment rates. This was accompanied by the problematization of youth unemployment, in which research perspectives competed to find the 'causes' of unemployment in either individual psychology or structural inequality. Sociologically oriented researchers emphasized the significance of social structures in young people's biographical pathways into (un) employment and critiqued policy interventions, such as government training schemes, as misguided attempts to solve structural problems through individualistic solutions. While there has been substantial theoretical development in the field of youth studies since Griffin's review was conducted, the basic issues at stake in this area remained remarkably consistent, focusing on structural inequalities in youth transitions and emphasizing structural explanations for youth unemployment. This remains the case despite shifts in the theoretical frameworks that have been drawn upon to construct this issue following the period of time covered by Griffin's review.

In the late 1990s, theoretical debates came to focus on the impact of the individualization thesis from theorists of late modernity such as Ulrich Beck (1992, 2000). The individualization thesis is a theory of social change that describes a shift from first to second modernity in terms of the fragmentation of the traditional structures of industrial society, such as the Fordist division of labour, unionized employment and the patriarchal nuclear family. These changes are driven by the deindustrialization of the global north, globalization and the impact of neoliberal employment policies, including the 'deregulation' of the labour market (although this will be interrogated in this book). As a result, the individualization thesis suggests that contemporary identities must be seen as reflexive, in which late modern subjects are forced to adopt an individualized and self-scrutinizing attitude towards their lives in order to navigate the structurally produced uncertainty that these social changes have created.

The impact of this theory on the sociology of youth was substantial, and the individualization thesis became the key theoretical touchstone for debates about youth transitions. The basic issues in these debates mirrored those of the 1970s and 1980s, focusing on the degree to which the individualization thesis emphasizes individual agency over structural inequality (Threadgold, 2011; Woodman, 2009; Roberts, 2012; and see Farrugia, 2013b for a review of these debates). The influential book by Furling and Cartmel (published in 1997 and updated in 2007) is a pivotal text in this area, critiquing the concept of reflexivity through evidence of the ongoing significance of structural inequalities for the social organization of young people's biographies. The individualization thesis also formed the basis for critiques of the concept of youth transitions as unnecessarily linear and incapable of grappling with complex social change (Andres and Wyn, 2010; Woodman and Wyn, 2015). In response, the concept of youth transitions was reasserted as the primary method for understanding structural inequalities in a context in which punitive and disciplinary approaches to unemployment remain the political norm (MacDonald, 2011). Throughout, the emphasis on pathways into employment as the critical focal point for understanding the relationship between young people and work has been taken for granted, and these transitions or biographical movements have been positioned as critical for understanding the social consequences of changing employment structures. In other words, assessments of the individualization thesis rehearse earlier debates about individualistic as opposed to structurally oriented approaches to youth transitions, and continue the key concerns of the transitions approach to youth.

This agenda has also failed to critique the assumption that young people's relationship with work should be examined from the perspective of the supply of labour to capital. It is taken for granted that the ideal situation for young people is to become employed, and that interventions into young people's lives should encourage this situation if possible, on the proviso that they are not punished for experiencing unemployment, which is a structural feature of the labour market. While young people undoubtedly live more fulfilling lives if they are or have a prospect of being securely employed, there are important aspects of the position of young people as economic subjects that are ignored here, including in particular the status of young people as workers who are compelled to produce value through labour, the processes of exploitation this entails and the broader processes of labour force formation that take place in the formation of productive workers (see Chapter 2 for an approach to this process from the perspective of post-Fordism). In this book, I address these issues through a focus on the formation of young people as workers, analysing the capacity for economic productivity as an aspect of youth subjectivities.

One of the implications of this shift is a new understanding of the way that social inequalities operate in young people's relationship with work. Contemporary social policies understand the resources that young people bring to the labour market through individualistic notions of human capital drawn essentially from neoclassical economics. In recent years, the concept of human capital has been increasingly associated with psychological and neuroscientific understandings of youth development, in which human capital accumulation is positioned as a quasi-natural developmental process taking place universally and supported ideally by free and deregulated markets (Farrugia, 2018a, pp 21–40). In contrast, sociologically oriented approaches to youth transitions foreground the structural distribution of resources according to social inequalities and the accumulation of advantage or disadvantage within institutions such as the education system. For example, this is what motivates critiques of the impact of 'educational inflation' on youth transitions (eg MacDonald, 2011), in which the labour market value of a degree decreases owing to the increase in the availability of graduates, motivating young people to pursue post-graduate study to achieve any level of employment security. What unites both of these approaches is the understanding that young people's engagement with work consists of the exchange of resources on the labour market in return for a wage reflecting market demand for their skills.

This is what Lisa Adkins (2005b) has described as the social contract view of work. In this approach, workers stand at a distance to the labour market, and then engage with it on the basis of resources they possess (such as property) and can deploy to their advantage (or disadvantage). This approach to the relationship between youth and work is limited by shifts in the relationship between work and the self to be discussed in Chapter 2, in which the self in general is becoming a source of value in ways that go beyond the possession of capitals. However, in sketching out the position of this book, what I want to emphasize is that a narrow focus on pathways through employment obscures the role of work as a site for subject formation in itself. In other words, it is not merely that young people approach work with different levels of resources, but rather that work and processes of labour force formation fundamentally constitute youth itself. Young people do not therefore stand at a distance to work and then engage with it, but rather are formed anew through the compulsion to become workers. In this book, I show that this includes the necessity of accumulating the capacity to produce value, and to cultivate the self in line with the disciplinary requirements of work.

Beyond false consciousness

While it has not made anything like the same kind of intellectual and social policy impact as the concept of youth transitions, the recently articulated political economy of youth (Cote, 2014) perspective has promised to address some of these concerns, and has sparked some debate in the sociology of youth (France and Threadgold, 2016). According to James Cote (2014), the political economy of youth perspective is aimed at situating youth within a framework that emphasizes the role of young workers in producing value and profit, and the exploitation of youth as a group by adult capitalists. In this way, the political economy of youth perspective situates youth as a class, in which the material conditions and relationships that define youth are analysed relative to adults, and in which the exploitation of youth is analysed in terms of how it enriches a particular segment of the adult population (ie the bourgeoisie). With this framework, Cote analyses increasing levels of inequality and the emergence of a super-rich '1 per cent' in terms of the increasing exploitation of young people, including the expansion of economic precarity and depressed wages on the part of the young. This is part of what Cote describes as the proletarianization of youth, or the creation of youth as a population and a labour force that operates primarily as a disempowered source of flexible labour for capital. Youth here is situated as a critical economic and political subject of contemporary capitalism, and young people are addressed as workers whose exploitation facilitates broader political economic relations and processes.

The political economy of youth perspective is valuable in that it situates youth as part of a theory of capitalism, including labour, value, exploitation and profit. Cote (2014) is certainly right when he argues that this is currently missing from the field, with some notable exceptions (eg Sukarieh and Tannock, 2014). Understanding youth in terms of a political economy also operates as a critique of youth studies perspectives that describe and celebrate young people's experiences without interrogating the material conditions that shape their capacities for action (Cote, 2014). A political economy perspective also draws attention to the wide array of elite actors that shape youth and that recruit concepts of youth into their own political projects, and therefore to the production of youth as a part of relationships between state, economy and society (Sukarieh and Tannock, 2016). In the process, the political economy of youth perspective goes beyond the perspective on inequality that underpins the notion of youth transitions. Instead of biographical inequalities emerging from the mobilization of resources on the labour market, the political economy of youth perspective situates youth as a group that is exploited as such, and that can therefore be understood relative to other groups such as adults (Cote, 2014) as well as to actors such as the state and other governmental authorities (Sukarieh and Tannock, 2014).

However, the political economy of youth perspective has also introduced a problematic account of young people's subjectivities as they relate to work. Within this perspective as it currently stands, youth subjectivities are analysed through a distinction between revolutionary potential and false consciousness. Essentially, young people are understood as a disenfranchised group who are prevented from seeing and working towards their own political and economic interests owing to the ideological forces of late capitalism. These ideological forces are diverse, and at least for Cote (2014) appear to include every identity practice that does not contribute to revolutionary social change. Youth cultures, all forms of cultural consumption and mediated entertainment are all included in this list, and blamed for the fact that young people do not see and act upon the revolutionary potential inherent in themselves as a proletarian class. Researchers that analyse youth subjectivities in themselves without reducing them to false or revolutionary consciousness are then positioned as contributing to liberal youth studies, and as being apologists for the exploitation of young people (France and Threadgold, 2016). In this way, the political economy perspective of youth reduces the study of subjectivity to assessments of the degree to which young people have been duped into acting against their own interests by the forces of consumerism and mediatized culture.

It is impossible to capture how youth subjectivities are formed in relation to the demands of the post-Fordist labour force through a distinction between false and revolutionary consciousness. First, this argument renders young people as cultural dupes (France and Threadgold, 2016), and relies on an essentialist approach to human subjectivity as containing an intrinsic revolutionary potential that is obfuscated by culture without analysing the actually existing subjectivities formed as part of the processes of capitalist valorization. Moreover, distinctions between false and revolutionary consciousness are blind to the enormously diverse and contradictory imperatives that currently shape the cultivation of the young working self. They will be discussed in more detail in Chapter 2, but include discourses of employability, soft skills and passionate commitments as aspects of ideal young workers, a late modern culture of self-realization that mandates an authentic personal commitment to work as a condition for success in life, and the emergence of forms of work in which the subjectivity of a worker is made critical to the value of labour and in which the intimate dimensions of the self are enrolled into the value that a subject offers to the labour force. Whether or not these experiences are 'false' in relation to an imagined essential revolutionary subject is less important here than understanding how young people respond to the imperatives to form the self as a worker, and the way that their identity practices constitute the nature of the post-Fordist labour force. That is the concern of this book.

The subjectification function of work

On the basis of my discussion so far, there are two key problems in contemporary studies of youth and work. The first is a focus on biographical transitions within the social contract view of labour, which positions work as a realm that young people transition into, rather than a site for the production of youth as such. This perspective assumes the perspective of the supply of labour to capital as the key imperative driving studies of youth and work, and neglects the formation of young people as workers within the dynamics of labour and subjectivity in contemporary capitalism. The second is a distinction between false and revolutionary consciousness in which the status of young people as economic subjects is assessed in relation to their material interests as identified in advance by researchers. This perspective renders actually existing working identities as uninteresting beyond their status as exemplars of false consciousness, itself defined as any meaningful practice that is not politically revolutionary. In this book, I want to move beyond both of these perspectives through a focus on what Kathi Weeks has called the 'subjectification function' of work (Weeks, 2011, p 8).

In her book *The Problem with Work*, Weeks (2011) explores and critically interrogates the role of work in the production of subjectivity in a general sense. For Weeks, capitalism is a 'work society', in which the subjectification function of work produces social relationships and subjectivities from the most public to the most intimate. Weeks describes the subjectification function of work when she argues that

> Work produces not just economic goods and services but also social and political subjects. In other words, the wage relation generates not just income and capital, but disciplined individuals, governable subjects, worthy citizens ... work constitutes a particularly important site for interpellation into a range of subjectivities. (Weeks, 2011, pp 8–9)

In other words – and in line with what I want to explore in this book – Weeks is suggesting that work is not merely a context that is entered into in order to receive a wage (as in the concept of youth transitions), but a critical site for the formation of subjectivities and social relations, and therefore for the operation of power relationships enacted through the most personal and intimate dimensions of the self. The formation of economic subjects takes place not only through engagement with the labour market on the part of a subject that exists prior to becoming a worker. Instead, what becomes visible here is the formation of the self in line with the social relations of employment and within the demands placed upon young people in the process of becoming a worker.

One of the key concepts introduced in Weeks's work is the post-Fordist work ethic. The post-Fordist work ethic is one of the key concepts that will be used in this book, and is explored in detail in Chapter 2. Briefly, Weeks's concept of the post-Fordist work ethic is a development and a new articulation of classical sociological thinking that began with the work of Max Weber on the Protestant work ethic, which Weber argued was a means of disciplining the early industrial working class by making salvation in the next life contingent on a total commitment to work as an end in itself during a worker's time on earth. However, the concept of the work ethic also explores how the subjectification function of work operates to produce labour forces that are specific to changing, historically specific forms of labour and regimes of value creation. For Weeks, the post-Fordist work ethic describes the subjectification function of work in an era in which notions of self-expression and authentic self-realization have become ethics of the self through which subjectivities are formed in line with the disciplinary requirements of work. More than merely a false consciousness, the post-Fordist work ethic describes what Weeks (2011, p 75) calls the 'ontological reward' of work, in which subjectivity itself is made contingent on the realization of the value of the self at work, and is therefore aligned with the value of the self to the labour force.

Moreover, and in an argument that resonates with existing concerns in studies of youth and work, Weeks's argument for work as a site for the interpellation of subjects focuses in particular on work as a site for class formation. Weeks argues that work is

> A key site of becoming classed ... Class identities and relations are made and remade as some people are excluded from and others conscripted into work, by means of educational tracks and workplace training regimens, through the organisation of labour processes and the interactions they structure, via the setting of wage levels, and in relation to judgments about occupational status ... Along these lines, one can observe that some of the attractions of different forms of work are about joining a relatively advantaged class: becoming a member of the working class rather than the underclass, a middle-class rather than a working class person, a salaried versus an hourly worker, a professional with a career as opposed to a working stiff and job holder. (Weeks, 2011, p 9)

For the purposes of understanding young people and work, Weeks's arguments here suggest that social class should be understood not merely in terms of the social distribution of resources (such as educational qualifications and skills) and their exchange on the labour market, but must instead be understood in terms of the production of classed inequalities through the intersection of institutional structures, labour relations and personal desires for meaningful and respected social status (ie subjectivities themselves). This means that the resources required to engage with the labour market are not separate from the self and possessed like property, but rather the classed self is constituted in the process of becoming a worker.

This is perhaps an uncontroversial claim. Class is often taken for granted as connected with work and labour relations, and there was for a period of time a substantial research tradition located primarily in the UK and US that examined work, class and identity, including the foundational work of Sennett and Cobb (1972) and E.P. Thompson (1980), and decades of research reviewed in Strangleman (2012, 2015). However, in recent years, work has shifted from the forefront of class research. The key reason for this is the dominance of what Savage (2003) has described as a 'new class paradigm' based on the work of Pierre Bourdieu (1984, 1990), in which the cultural politics of neoliberalism has replaced work and labour as the key site for the formation of classed subjectivities. Bourdieu's work has been enormously influential in the sociology of youth, and the next section of this chapter explores the consequences of a Bourdieusian approach to class for understanding work in ways that are both sympathetic to and critical of the implications of Bourdieusian theory.

Class and work beyond Bourdieu

The work of Pierre Bourdieu has arguably become the single most dominant approach to social class in Anglophone sociology and is perhaps the only coherent theoretical approach to class currently in use in the sociology of youth. Bourdieu's work forms the basis for new models of social inequality, including the Great British Class Survey (Savage, 2003; Savage et al, 2013) which created typologies of social class consisting of seven categories ranging from a wealthy elite, an affluent professional middle class, new forms of technical experts and affluent workers, to three categories of working-class and precariously employed workers. However, what is particularly critical for my purposes here is that Bourdieusian theory has also brought subjectivity to the fore of class research. In particular, the work of authors such as Skeggs (1997, 2004), Lawler (2005) and Tyler (2013) on the cultural politics of class, gender and neoliberalism has been enormously influential throughout sociology and has had a substantial impact on the sociology of youth (Allen and Hollingworth, 2013; France and Threadgold, 2016; Threadgold, 2018).

In a nutshell, Bourdieu's (1990) approach to social class focuses on the way that distinction or prestige is attributed to differently positioned subjects within economies of symbolic value formed through social struggle. Bourdieu describes the world as made up of 'fields', or systems of objective structural relations defined by distributions of 'cultural capital', a term that describes the symbolic resources available to classed subjects to participate in the structural environment of fields. What counts as cultural capital is an outcome of social struggles over meaning and value in which differently positioned groups aim to have their identities, tastes and lifestyles defined as legitimate and valuable. The creation of classed subjectivities takes place in this context through the formation of the 'habitus', which describes a series of embodied dispositions towards the meaning of the social world and to the objective possibilities for action available to differently positioned subjects. Classed subjectivities are therefore defined by their position within fields and their stocks of available cultural capital, which is mobilized according to the dispositions of the habitus. Distinction takes place when symbolic capital is realized through recognition by the habitus, which tends to 'mis-recognize' capitals as attributes of individuals rather than of social structures, and therefore confers prestige and legitimacy on the domination of dominant groups.

Among the most significant uptakes of Bourdieu's work has been the work of feminist scholars, who have developed the implications of Bourdieu's original work to place matters of subjectivity, embodiment, affect and taste at the centre of class research. This has drawn attention to what Reay (2005) has described as the 'psychic landscape' of class, or the lived experiences of distinction and denigration that make up the affective dimensions of class. Lawler (2005) and Tyler (2013, 2015) have described the way that power relationships and classed subjectivities are produced through definitions of worth and worthlessness that reflect neoliberal notions of individualized failure and success. These hierarchies of value are experienced in terms of shame and disgust that reflect the misrecognition of capital within the cultural politics of neoliberalism. Skeggs (2005, 2011) describes classed subjectivities as formed through an incitement to understand the self as a value-accruing individual, in which the requirement to accumulate symbolic value operates as an 'ethical scenario' (Skeggs, 2005, p 973) for the formation of the classed self. In this sense, Bourdieu's emphasis on the accumulation and contestation of symbolic capital is for Skeggs not merely a generic attribute of the relationship between habitus and field, but takes a particular form through the dynamics of class in neoliberalism. In general, this body of literature has become foundational to contemporary studies of class and has shown how classed power relationships are enacted through cultural politics and embodied subjectivity.

Bourdieu's work has had an enormous impact throughout the sociology of youth and cognate fields, such as the sociology of education (Ball, 1993; Ball et al, 2000; Andres and Wyn, 2010; Threadgold, 2018). France and Threadgold (2016) have drawn on Bourdieu to critique the notion of youth as a class plagued by false consciousness, as articulated in the political economy of youth perspective. Their work draws attention to the varied distributions of symbolic capital to be found *within* the youth segment, as well as the production of difference as a result of meaningful cultural and identity practices that reflect broader symbolic economies but do not rely on a model of youth as cultural dupes. In debates about youth transitions, Bourdieu's work has long been used as a foil for the individualization thesis and the concept of reflexivity (Woodman, 2009), with references to habitus used to explain the ongoing existence of class inequalities among young people in conditions of social change. The uses of Bourdieu's work here range in the extent of their implications, from an emphasis on social reproduction (Brannen and Nilsen, 2005) to a discussion of the way that reflexive practices are shaped by dispositions (Threadgold and Nilan, 2009; Farrugia, 2013a). More recently, Bourdieu's work has been used in innovative ways to understand how modes of youth distinction are enacted through popular culture (Threadgold, 2018), and underpins analysis of class privilege among young people (France et al, 2018). There is also an extensive tradition of Bourdieusian work examining the way that classed subjectivities are formed within education, which explores the devalorization of working-class students in schools and universities. In Reay's (2005) work, working-class students described feeling that they were positioned as 'nothing' within educational institutions that valorized middle-class trajectories and norms of bodily comportment and aesthetics. In general, therefore, Bourdieusian approaches to class have had an enormous impact on the sociology of youth, shaping debates about youth transitions and tracing new relationships between youth subjectivities and contemporary cultural politics.

However, the use of Bourdieu to understand the relationship between youth and work remains an open question. Work is not a key concern for Bourdieu, and the upsurge of interest in him has been primarily focused on cultural politics or the structuring of youth transitions. Within a Bourdieusian framework, work is significant inasmuch as it positions social groupings within broader economies of cultural capital and shapes the position that people occupy within different fields. Occupational hierarchies and statuses are a critical aspect of Bourdieu's analysis, but they operate to shape people's trajectories within social space and are not examined as sites for the formation of subjectivities themselves. The development of new models of social stratification based on Bourdieu's work that are described in Savage et al (2013) therefore share this problem: occupational groups contribute to the organization of structural inequalities, but are represented in terms of constellations of consumption practices that contribute to the prestige associated with classed groupings, rather than in terms of the subjectification function of work. So, while the increasing influence of Bourdieu in studies of youth has led to productive theoretical debates about how to understand inequality, the utility of Bourdieusian concepts for understanding class and work remains an open question.

Research on young people and deindustrialization has made some progress in this regard. Anoop Nayak (2006) has drawn on Bourdieu to describe how an industrial working-class masculine habitus is transformed or reproduced when manual labour is no longer available, and has shown how distinctions between the respectable and rough working class are expressed through new forms of labour and consumption. Ciaran Burke (2016) has explored class distinctions in the way that graduates engage with the labour market to show how the possession of cultural capital facilitates the cultivation of employability across a graduate's lifestyle in ways that go beyond the possession of a degree. This is opposed to the strategies of working-class students, whose lack of knowledge of the 'rules of the game' of graduate employability leads to strategies that are limited to attaining formal credentials, ultimately reproducing their relatively disempowered position within the graduate labour force. Historical and contemporary studies of work, class and identity also share many of the concerns that Bourdieusian theorists have foregrounded in their analyses of the cultural politics of class, in which the subjective experience of hierarchies of value and prestige are enacted through work. For example, research focusing on industrial and post-industrial workers, such as Sennett and Cobb (1972) and Lamont (2000), has focused on the ambivalent and contradictory affective and subjective experiences produced through performing devalorized working class work in a social context that encourages aspiration and social mobility. These include feelings of shame, pride, dignity, aspiration and frustration, all reflected in experiences of labour processes, workplace hierarchies and relations, and broader social relationships in which the nature, status and affective experience of work impacts upon a worker's relationship with their families and friends. These studies have demonstrated the critical significance of work in what Sayer (2005) calls the moral dynamics of class, or the attribution of moral value to classed subjects. These relationships – between moral value, affective experiences, social relationships and structural conditions – are critical to Bourdieusian analyses of symbolic value, distinction and subjectivity, and act as an important reminder of the importance of work to class analysis after Bourdieu.

Therefore, while Bourdieu has contributed to the invisibility of work in contemporary class research (though see Burke, 2016; Roberts, 2018; Burke et al, 2019), there are elements of this approach that I want to develop here as ways of understanding the formation of young people as workers in contemporary or post-Fordist economies. In particular, Bourdieusian perspectives on class have introduced a useful consideration of value as an attribute of subjectivities. The work of Bev Skeggs (2004, 2005, 2011) is at the forefront of these discussions, exploring how notions of value, property and personhood have become intertwined. Skeggs argues that economic value is moralized as a reflection of propriety, a moral value assigned to a self-possessed subject for whom notions of property define the relation of the self to the self and to others. In this way, subjectivities become suffused with notions of value operating according to an economic logic, while the relational and affective practices that are considered non-economic (such as care for others) are rendered invisible or devalorized. This theorization of notions of value as dimensions of the classed self is useful for understanding the formation of productive subjects; that is, of subjects for which the capacity to produce value is a critical attribute of their personal identity. Moreover, and in a more general sense, Bourdieu's effort to combine Weberian notions of social status with Marxist and other structuralist analyses of material relationships could be useful for understanding the cultivation of the productive self as a realm for the creation of class distinction. This is especially the case if – as will be argued in Chapter 2 – the aspects of identity now enrolled into the cultivation of the self as a worker are becoming increasingly expansive. If more and more of the self is now mobilized in becoming productive, then the role of work in the production of classed distinctions takes on a new significance.

This book therefore broadens understandings of classed subjectivities beyond economies of symbolic value, and towards the cultivation of the self as a subject of value to the labour force. This includes the role of social class in shaping the practices mobilized by differently positioned young people in forming identities as workers and understanding themselves as productive subjects. This perspective is at some distance from the way that class inequality is understood in notions of youth transitions, which is essentially based on a social contract view of work in which resources are exchanged for wages and conditions. Rather than a subject that exchanges unequally distributed resources in the marketplace, this book understands classed subjectivity itself as produced in the process of becoming a worker. In this respect, it is necessarily intertwined with the value generation mechanisms that shape the youth labour force in post-Fordism, especially those connected with the expansion of the disciplinary requirements of work to all areas of the contemporary self. In Chapter 2, I develop this perspective further in relation to existing concerns with reflexivity, practice and the post-Fordist work ethic.

Overview and project summary

The empirical portions of this book draw on a programme of research conducted with young people living in two geographical areas that were characterized by comparatively high levels of youth unemployment and rapid labour market transformations over the last three decades. Between 2016 and 2017, I conducted biographical interviews with 74 young people aged between 17 and 29 (44 young women and 33 young men) at school, in further training, working or unemployed, and from a diverse range of class backgrounds. In 2017 and 2018, I interviewed 11 of these participants a second time in order to explore whether and how their experiences over the course of the project had changed their perspectives and attitudes towards work. This is indicated when relevant in the analysis, although most of the data in this book comes from the first round of interviews. Interviews discussed young people's experiences of work, the value that they felt they held to the labour force, their hopes and aspirations for the future, and the relationship between their experiences of work and other parts of their lives.

As Kenway et al (2006) have shown, local economic transformations impact on young people in ways that reflect the history of their localities. Young people attribute meaning and value to work at the nexus of changing expectations about the role of work in a young person's life and about what constitutes good and meaningful work for differently positioned youth in a particular local context. With this in mind, the two research sites were chosen for the way that the nature of work has changed over time, as well as representing what at the time were called 'youth unemployment hotspots' (BSL, 2014). While the project was concerned with working identities as much as with experiences of unemployment, these research sites provided a powerful insight into the way that local economic histories and transformations impacted upon young people in different ways. One research site was Newcastle, Australia – a city located around two hours' drive from Sydney, the capital city of New South Wales. Sampling also included the peri-urban surrounds of this city. Newcastle has undergone substantial economic changes in the last three decades that are representative of the deindustrialization of the global north taking place during that time. Once home to a substantial steel refinery providing much of the area's employment, the city is now transitioning to a mixed economy composed of professional and consumer services as well as primary industry, owing to a large and productive coal-mining region nearby. The other site – Mildura – is a rural city in western Victoria with an economy consisting of horticulture, professional and consumer services, and welfare services. It is regarded (and was described by locals) as a disadvantaged city with a persistently high level of youth out-migration owing to the absence of substantial educational and work opportunities in the local area. The design therefore provides a sensitivity to the contemporary significance of place amid changes in the nature and social organization of work (Farrugia, 2018a), in particular the impact of local labour markets and economic histories on young people's working identities (Kenway et al, 2006; Farrugia, 2013b).

The data in Chapters 3, 4 and 5 explore narratives about work, productivity, value and the self. The empirical analysis is organized according to three ideal typical categories that emerged inductively from the analysis, discussed in one chapter each. Each chapter describes how young people imagined themselves as productive subjects, the practices that young people employed to cultivate a productive self, their definitions of failure and success, and the projects of self-formation that they pursued. In the process, class is not analysed as an a priori, but rather as a form of subjectivity that is produced through young people's identity practices. Nevertheless, the categories discussed in Chapters 3 and 4 reflected distinctions between young people from family backgrounds including higher education and professional employment, and young people from family backgrounds including trades and clerical employment with varying levels of post-compulsory education. Chapter 5 discusses young people who had experienced substantial periods of unemployment and marginalization, who were either from backgrounds in which their parents had experienced disability or substantial unemployment themselves, or were from families similar to those discussed in Chapter 4 (none were from middle-class families). Chapter 5 therefore discusses both the experience of substantial marginalization and the way that experiences of unemployment impact on the meaning of work and the cultivation of the working self. In what remains of this chapter, I summarize each of these chapters in turn in order to provide a guide for the remainder of the book.

Outline of the book

Chapter 2 of this book explores the relationship between youth and post-Fordism, and in this way offers a theoretical framework for understanding the cultivation of the self as a subject of value to the labour force. The chapter describes the nature of post-Fordism from the perspective of the relationship between subjectivity and value. This includes a review of concept of immaterial labour, the conversion of life itself into post-Fordist value and the collapse of work into the self. In this context, the chapter argues that post-Fordism and immaterial labour align the self with the logic of value in new ways, but create questions about the practices through which the self as value is cultivated. These questions also relate to the way in which differently positioned young people relate to the requirement to craft the self as a worker in line with the demands of post-Fordist work. With this in mind, the chapter explores the post-Fordist work ethic as a way of understanding the practices and ethics through which young people are formed as workers. This includes a discussion of the classed history of the work ethic. This history is more complex than epochal periodizations between Fordist and post-Fordist capitalism would necessarily allow, but nevertheless offers a useful and generative framework for understanding the formation of young people as workers in relation to the subjectivities of the post-Fordist labour force. The chapter concludes by exploring how to account for the practices through which young people become subjects of the work ethic.

Chapter 3 is the first of three empirical chapters describing how the post-Fordist work ethic produces youth subjectivities. Each of these chapters describes an ideal typical manifestation of the subjectivities produced by the post-Fordist work ethic, including the relationship between value and the self, the practices used to cultivate the self as a subject of value to the labour force, and the forms of identity and self-realization that are (or are not) produced through these practices. In particular, Chapter 3 describes middle-class 'subjects of passion', and theorizes the ethic of passion as a way in which young people craft the post-Fordist self. In a nutshell, subjects of passion understand the entirety of their lives as contributing to the value of the self as a worker and mobilize what they describe as passionate affects across the whole of their life in the formation of the working self. Because subjects of passion understand their value to the labour force in terms of the totality of their personal affectivities, there is no limit to the practices they consider to be relevant in the cultivation of the working self. These practices therefore include anything that cultivates the passion of the subject and can include leisure activities and other forms of sociality not usually recognized as productive or connected with employability. For subjects of passion, work is a realm for self-actualization through the realization of these passionate commitments, which are described as both the source of value and the ultimate purpose of work. For this reason, subjects of passion are the ideal post-Fordist subjects, enrolling the entirety of their lives and subjectivities into the formation of themselves as workers.

Chapter 4 describes aspirational working-class 'subjects of achievement', who also approach work as a realm of self-actualization, but for whom the relationship between value and the self, and the practices used to cultivate the value of the self, are different in critical ways to those of subjects of passion. For subjects of achievement, the aim of work is social mobility and material security – topics that are remote to the narratives from subjects of passion. Subjects of achievement understand the value of the self not in terms of passion but in terms of competence – a personal attribute that predisposes one to be 'good at' a specific realm of labour, and that can be cultivated into skills through work experience or education. In the ethic of achievement, a young person must reflexively identify something that they are good at and cultivate this into a skill, with material rewards to follow. Self-realization therefore means the realization of competence into value, manifested by social mobility. For this reason, the practices included in the formation of the self as a worker are restricted to those that cultivate competence (as opposed to subjects of passion, for whom these practices were almost limitless). In their emphasis on social mobility as a reflection of the realization of competence, subjects of achievement reflect the history of the work ethic, intertwining Fordist and post-Fordist modes of subjectification in a contemporary manifestation of the self as value.

Chapter 5 describes young people whose identities as workers are abject to the forms of self-realization offered (and mandated) in the ethics of passion and achievement. The chapter describes those for whom experiences of unemployment, alienating labour and marginalization has meant that work is not a realm of self-realization but rather of precarity and degradation. In this chapter, young people experiencing substantial periods of unemployment describe experiencing work as an unfamiliar world in which they are forced to conform to affective and relational styles that must be learned deliberately in order to project the image of an appropriately disciplined worker in order to find work. Rather than authentic self-realization, these young people are focused on 'getting it right' in the presentation of themselves as socially appropriate workers, while also experiencing the humiliation of being rejected in job interviews and intensely governed by welfare authorities. In this context, the meaning of work is not self-realization but material survival, and the protection of the self from the inevitable injuries of precarious work and unemployment. Chapter 5 therefore reveals the post-Fordist promise of self-realization through work as a myth that produces experiences of devalorization and abjection in the most marginal parts of the youth labour market.

Chapter 6 concludes the book by interrogating concepts of post-Fordism and the post-Fordist work ethic and exploring what these concepts mean for the sociology of youth and work. The chapter complicates suggestions about the conversion of life itself into value and about the collapse of work into the self, both of which have become part of discussions about post-Fordism. In this context, the chapter argues that the relationship between identity, productivity and value is enacted differently in different manifestations of the work ethic, making the notion that subjectivity in general has collapsed into work inadequate for understanding the formation of young people as workers. Instead, the post-Fordist work ethic must be understood as heterogeneous and as inflected by processes of class distinction that create different relationships between value and the self. These relationships also amount to different forms of exploitation that are facilitated by the post-Fordist work ethic. Value is extracted from young people's subjectivities through different relationships to work that are themselves organized through processes of class distinction that take place through the work ethic. This distinction is intertwined with the experience of valorization or denigration at work and in experiences of unemployment. The chapter concludes with an argument for situating youth within theories of post-Fordism and outlining future directions in the study of education, labour processes and employment politics.

After this conclusion, I provide a short methodological afterword for readers interested in the analytic process that led to the arguments and structure of the book. This afterword engages with Weber's notion of ideal types and explains the relevance of this concept for understanding the formation of young people as workers. In particular, I make a case for the usefulness and necessity of clear ideal/typical concepts as opposed to recent calls for 'mess' in social science research and describe the process that led to the conceptual logic of the book. This short chapter details the key analytical relationships that I focused on in order to create the book's framework and to pursue its overall project. Having made this clear, the chapter then explores a participant whose biography and approach to work complicates the framework developed in the previous chapters. By exploring a participant who is 'between' the ethics of the self described earlier, I show how the ambivalence experienced by a single young person can be understood in terms of contradictions within the post-Fordist work ethic itself.

Conclusion

In summary, the aim of this book is to explore the formation of young people as workers as an aspect of the relationship between work and the self in post-Fordism. The concept of the post-Fordist work ethic situates youth itself as a product of the subjectification function of work, while a focus on biographical practices means that the relationship between class and post-Fordist subjectivities can be subjected to empirical scrutiny. In this way, the following pages explore the practices through which the youth labour force is formed in its classed dimensions, and the biopolitical terrain on which young people become productive subjects. Youth subjectivities are thereby positioned within the dynamics of labour, productivity and value creation. Chapter 2 establishes the theoretical framework for the book by exploring the position of youth within post-Fordism and the post-Fordist work ethic.

2

Youth in the New Economy: The Post-Fordist Self

This book explores the formation of youth identities in terms of the cultivation of the self as a subject of value to the labour force. This chapter builds the conceptual framework that underpins this focus, which will be used to situate young people within the dynamics of work and subjectivity in contemporary capitalism. The chapter is divided into four sections. The first establishes the conceptual utility of concepts connected to post-Fordism for understanding the relationship between youth and work, focusing in particular on shifts in the social organization of employment, the nature of labour and the relationship between labour, value and the self. The second section describes Kathi Weeks's concept of the post-Fordist work ethic, which theorizes historical shifts in the meaning of work in different phases of capitalism, beginning with the work of Weber and developing into a discussion of the ethical relationship to work mandated in post-Fordism. The third section explores the way that young people are positioned within the dynamics of post-Fordist work, arguing that youth has become critical to post-Fordist capitalism, operating both as an important source of value and as a point of intervention for governmental efforts aiming to craft and manage a labour force. Finally, the chapter describes what is meant by the cultivation of the self as a subject of value, in the context of the social transformations of post-Fordism and disciplinary requirements imposed by the post-Fordist work ethic.

In the process, the chapter aims to make a number of conceptual shifts in the concepts and theoretical narratives most influential in framing young people's relationship with work. The first and most significant is a shift away from narratives relying on the concept of late modernity and towards an exploration of shifts in the nature of capitalism. While these terms are perhaps not mutually exclusive, notions of late modernity rely on generic narratives about individualized subjectivities to be found across all aspects of social life, while the value of narratives of post-Fordism is to foreground the social and biopolitical conditions that shape the formation of labouring subjectivities within the disciplinary requirements of contemporary work. Following this renewed focus on post-Fordist capitalism, the chapter aims to move beyond generic notions of reflexivity in the sociology of youth to examine how the biopolitics of work exemplified by the post-Fordist work ethic mandates a particular ethical relation to the self in the process of becoming a worker. The cultivation of the self as a worker is therefore understood not merely as a form of biographical work, but as a specific relationship to the self that is required of young people in anticipating a position within the labour force. The shift here, therefore, is away from notions of individualization and reflexivity as generic features of late modern subjectivities and towards a consideration of work as a realm with specific, historically contingent disciplinary requirements for subject formation that run parallel with the dynamics of labour and value in post-Fordist capitalism.

Post-Fordism and the new economy

This section describes an approach to the relationship between youth, work and the self that is inspired by theories connected with post-Fordism, or more broadly what has been referred to as the 'new economy' (Adkins, 2005b). The section draws on notions of post-Fordism (Amin, 2003), 'immaterial labour' (Lazzarato, 1996) and broader discussions about work and the self in the new economy (Adkins and Lury, 1999; Adkins, 2005b) to theorize the formation of the young working self in terms of the relationship between value and subjectivity in contemporary capitalism.

As discussed in Chapter 1, the two approaches to youth, work and the self currently at issue in the sociology of youth are the political economy of youth perspective and the transitions approach developed through an engagement with theories of late modernity. The political economy of youth approach is articulated against 'liberal' approaches that are diverse but include theories of social change. In this account, what counts is the 'business as usual' of exploitation under capitalism, the fundamental dynamics of which Cote (2014) claims have not changed beyond an increase in inequality and exploitation owing to neoliberalism. In contrast, theories of late modernity position changes in the social organization of work within a shift from 'first' to 'second' modernity, in which the 'heavy' social structures of industrial societies give way to the light or 'liquid' (Bauman, 2000) conditions to be found in late modernity. In first modernity, unionized manufacturing labour underpinned structures such as the patriarchal nuclear family and facilitated relatively straightforward movements from education into work such as those described in the canonical work of Willis (1977), in which working-class boys got working-class jobs in a relatively predictable manner. Indeed, Willis's (1977) work can be read as an account of the formation of young workers in Fordist capitalism, which took place at the intersection of local employment structures, education systems and modes of working-class masculinity that valorized attributes connected with the culture of the shop floor. For Willis, industrial male workers were formed through ethics that celebrated tough masculinity and collective solidarities expressed in 'piss-taking', while young men rarely aspired to jobs of a higher status or level of remuneration than their fathers.

The shift to liquid modernity describes the dissolution of these structural relationships (between work, family and youth biographies) as a result of a range of processes that include globalization and the deindustrialization of the global north, in which unionized work in manufacturing is replaced by precarious work in consumer services as the key destination for working-class youth. In an early discussion of individualization, Beck (1992) describes these changes in terms of the inevitable logic of the capitalist labour market, in which workers are necessarily positioned as individuals, leading to the fragmentation of social bonds connected with work. The consequence is increasing structurally produced uncertainty both in the realm of employment and in other areas, such as family life and intimate relationships, which must be navigated in an individualized and reflexive manner. In later work, Beck (2000) also suggests that late modern identities were less and less dependent on work, and that employment now formed part of a broader, reflexively constructed biographical identity also composed of multiple other lifestyle arenas.

Post-Fordist thinkers share a concern with precarity that is also raised by authors writing within concepts of late modernity, and the concern with labour, value and profit in the political economy of youth approach. However, rather than reflexivity or false consciousness, notions of post-Fordism explore the complex relationship between the intimate dimensions of the self and the logic of work, and are made sensitive to social change through a focus on the disciplinary requirements of labour. The concept of post-Fordism is part of discussions of a 'new economy' (Adkins, 2005b), in which changes in the social organization of production and value accumulation take place alongside a shift in the relationship between subjectivity and work, such that the self is increasingly produced, experienced and performed through the disciplinary requirements of work. The concept of post-Fordism has been impactful in a range of disciplinary areas that I will not review in detail here, but which include political economy, political science, geography and sociology (Amin, 2003). My use of the term is drawn primarily from a body of work that argues the creation of subjectivity should be analysed in terms of the requirements of capitalist valorization, including a significant body of work on gender and the new economy (McRobbie, 2011; Adkins and Dever, 2016) as well as the work of autonomous Marxists (Lazzarato, 1996; Hardt and Negri, 2004). In general, therefore, the concept of post-Fordism is here used to facilitate a consideration of the biopolitics of work, or the social arrangements and power relationships through which contemporary subjects are constituted as workers, and the techniques or so-called technologies of the self through which they are constituted as such through their own practices (Foucault, 1988; 2004).

One significant contribution of post-Fordist thinking is summed up in arguments for 'immaterial' or 'affective' labour as ways of capturing the impact of changes in the nature of work in the economies of the global north. In particular, these concepts foreground the economic centrality of service, knowledge and culture economies, in which labour involves the production of information, signs, symbols, affects, relationships and modes of cultural representation. These immaterial economies rely on a new relationship between work, value and subjectivity that has become general throughout much of the economy. In particular, immaterial labour describes the dissolution of the boundaries between what is and what is not labour, between work and non-work time, and between production and consumption. The reason for this is that immaterial production takes place not on the basis of skills that are exchanged on the labour market, but rather enrols subjectivity in its most general sense into the process of labour and value creation. Immaterial labour draws on a worker's basic capacities for relationality, empathy, embodiment and performativity in the course of the work, and therefore implicates a worker's entire subjectivity into the moment of labour. In the process, practices taking place outside work that contribute to these capacities are implicated in the formation of the working self, and the distinction between the productive and unproductive dimensions of the self becomes more difficult to sustain. For theorists of immaterial labour, there is no part of social life that is not somehow implicated in the economy within modes of production that create value from life itself (Hardt and Negri, 2004).

If theorists of immaterial labour are correct that this relationship between subjectivity and economy has become general throughout the economy, then this makes the social contract view of work that drives existing approaches to youth impossible to sustain. As I foreshadowed in Chapter 1, the social contract view of work is based on the assumption that young people confront the labour market possessed of skills and resources that produce value in their exchange for a wage. However, as Lisa Adkins (2005b) has argued, post-Fordist economies require not merely the ownership of particular skills or capitals, but rather aim to make the entire subjectivity of a worker into a source of productivity. The capacity for productivity is therefore not owned by a particular worker, but is rather a property of the 'multitude', a term that Hardt and Negri (2004) use to describe the productive capacities of life in its most general sense. This means that in post-Fordism it is not enough to examine the social distribution of resources that facilitate labour market advantage. The task is to examine how subjectivity is made productive across the whole of life, including areas that are not usually considered relevant to work. This is a contemporary example of what Kathi Weeks, discussed in Chapter 1, describes as the 'subjectification function' of work (Weeks, 2011, p 8), or the biopolitical practices through which working subjectivities are produced.

While these narratives about post-Fordist transformation are useful for creating new perspectives on the formation of the working self, they also raise new questions that go beyond the scope of existing theories. These questions relate to the issue of difference, inequality and the specific practices through which the self is formed in line with the demands of productivity. In this context, post-Fordist transformations such as those discussed here have been both generative and subject to substantial critique, especially in feminist discussions of the way that gender is implicated in the creation of value (Gill and Pratt, 2008; McRobbie, 2011; Adkins and Dever, 2016). In particular, it is not clear how the claim that life itself is the basis for productivity contributes to discussions about classed and gendered power relations within post-Fordist capitalism. Gill and Pratt (2008) argue that the notion of immaterial or affective labour lacks coherence, collapsing wildly different working subjectivities into the figure of a generic immaterial worker that is neither gendered nor classed, thereby limiting understandings of how differently positioned subjects are enrolled into different kinds of post-Fordist work. This is as a result of the failure on the part of autonomist Marxists to recognize that many of their assertions were made some decades ago by socialist feminists critiquing masculinist definitions of productivity and labour based on public/private binaries that divested women of their status as economic subjects (Jarrett, 2015). It is also as a result of Hardt and Negri's (2004) account of precarity, which they suggest has become such a general economic condition as to make hierarchical class analysis obsolete – a claim that appears rather remote to the different levels of employment security experienced by professional and managerial workers as opposed to those in consumer services (Bolton, 2009), as well as to the increasingly polarized employment conditions actually experienced by contemporary young people (Furlong et al, 2017). There is therefore a need to go beyond abstract generalizations about the productivity of subjectivity in general to consider how differently positioned subjects are responding to the demands of post-Fordist work.

Moreover – and in part as a response to this critique – it is also necessary to understand the particular practices through which differently positioned young people are actually formed as workers, and the way those practices are socially organized throughout young people's lives. The assertion that subjectivity in general or life itself is enrolled into the formation of workers is provocative of new and more expansive agendas in understanding the working self, but it provides no insight into the mechanisms through which the 'self in general' is made productive. If subjectivity itself is increasingly aligned with processes of valorization, what are the specific practices or, in Foucauldian terms, technologies of the self (Foucault, 1988) through which subjectivities and social relationships are mobilized in the formation of the self as a worker? In other words, what do young people actually do in their lives and what relationship to the self do they enact when they create an understanding of themselves as a subject of value to the labour force? Moreover, how do these practices contribute to the production of difference and inequalities within the formation of young people as workers? What are the relations of poverty and privilege enacted as young people construct a working self? These are the kinds of questions raised by framing the question of youth, identity and work in terms of the construction of the post-Fordist self, and it is in this way that this book will subject claims made in theories of post-Fordism to empirical scrutiny.

In general therefore, post-Fordist societies are characterized by the call to 'become somebody' by becoming a worker, and by an increased pressure to make all aspects of one's life productive and of value to the labour force. The post-Fordist working subject does not then merely approach the labour market with skills for sale, but is rather produced as an embodied, relational subject through engagement with work. I will subject these claims to some empirical scrutiny in the chapters that follow. However, I have also suggested that subjectivities are produced and regulated through the disciplinary requirements of post-Fordist work. In the next section of this chapter, I expand on this claim by exploring the disciplinary requirements of work through the lens of the post-Fordist work ethic. This concept provides a historical account of the way that the meaning of work has changed in different eras of capitalism, suggesting that different economic arrangements are accompanied by ideologically powerful but changing mandates about the role of work in a subject's life and relationship to the self.

The post-Fordist work ethic

Kathi Weeks's (2011) theorization of the post-Fordist work ethic provides an insight into how the disciplinary requirements of work are enacted in the production of subjectivities, and explores the ethical relationship to the self that is mandated in the process of becoming a worker in different eras of capitalism. Weeks's work therefore shows how the subjectification function of work operates, the specific form that it takes in different historical periods, the particular subjectivities produced through the work ethic and the way in which these subjectivities are enacted. Weeks also shows that in capitalist societies work occupies a uniquely powerful role in the creation of subjectivity. In different eras, work has offered promises of religious salvation, social mobility and self-actualization to subjects if only they would submit themselves fully to work and to the disciplinary requirements of becoming a worker. In this sense, Weeks's discussion of the post-Fordist work ethic introduces a new perspective on the formation of workers that focuses on the relationship of the self to the self that is mandated by the subjectification function of work, as well as the unique personal rewards that work is said to offer to those who devote themselves to becoming a worker.

We live – argues Weeks – in a work society, in which the necessity and moral and social significance of work has become entirely naturalized so as to appear inevitable. Work operates as the primary way in which people are integrated into social systems and relationships. Work is how we acquire the basic material necessities of life and is a critical source of sociality. Creating subjects that are capable of and willing to work is the primary goal of education systems, and raising children who can secure employment that will at least reproduce if not exceed the class position of parents is regarded as the 'gold standard' of parenting (Weeks, 2011, p 6). Work readiness is invoked to justify the nature of education systems, prison and justice facilities, and interventions into the physical and mental health of populations. Weeks argues that in capitalist societies characterized by an abundance of material resources and an unequal distribution of wealth, work must be understood in terms of the disciplinary requirements associated with 'becoming a worker':

> Work is, thus, not just an economic practice. Indeed, that every individual is required to work, that most are expected

to work for wages or be supported by someone who does, is a social convention and disciplinary apparatus rather than an economic necessity. That every individual must not only do some work but more often a lifetime of work, that individuals must not only work but become workers, is not necessary to the production of social wealth. (Weeks, 2011, pp 7–8)

In other words, the work society mandates work, and positions work as the central justification for a myriad of significant social institutions and relationships. However, it is not enough merely to work – one must *become a worker*. That is, it is through dedicating the self to work that we take on the status of socially and politically intelligible subjects:

> working is part of what is supposed to transform subjects into the independent individuals of the liberal imaginary, and for that reason, is treated as a basic obligation of citizenship … In other words, the wage relation generates not just income and capital, but disciplined individuals, governable subjects, worthy citizens and responsible family members. (Weeks, 2011, pp 8–9)

In this context, Weeks suggests that work should be understood through the lens of ethical obligation, and as a personal practice through which the moral norms of the work society are enacted:

> Work is not just defended on grounds of economic necessity and social duty; it is widely understood as an individual moral practice and collective ethical obligation. Traditional work values – those that preach the moral value and dignity of waged work and privilege such work as an essential source of individual growth, self-fulfilment, social recognition, and status – continue to be effective in encouraging and rationalising the long hours … workers are supposed to dedicate to waged work and the identities they are expected to invest there. (Weeks, 2011, p 11)

In general therefore, Weeks's discussion of the work society – and the distinction between working and the personal practices and ethical commitments driving the process of becoming a worker – emphasizes that throughout the history of capitalism, the compulsory nature of work goes beyond material necessity and reflects the political/moral dimensions of subjectivity and citizenship. However, Weeks's discussion of the post-Fordist work ethic is also aimed at historicizing this process, suggesting that the moral significance and ethical practices through which the self is converted into a worker have changed as a result of transformations in the nature of capitalism. While the subjectification function of work is constant throughout, what it means to become a worker reflects shifts in the social organization and nature of labour, and in the way that class relationships operate in this context. Weeks argues that

> The [work] ethic's consistent prescriptions for our identification with and constant devotion to work, its elevation of work as the rightful center of life, and its affirmation of work as an end in itself all help to produce the kinds of workers and the labouring capacities adequate to the contemporary regime of accumulation and the specific modes of social labour in which it invests. (Weeks, 2011, p 75)

For Weeks, understanding the role of work in producing the post-Fordist self begins with the classic account from Max Weber. For Weber, the Protestant work ethic was articulated as part of a pressing need to create a capitalist labour force from an often recalcitrant population used to the seasonal rhythms of agricultural labour. In this context, early proponents of the Protestant work ethic described a total ethical commitment to work as necessary for salvation in the next life, and success in work as a signifier of such salvation. Ironically, the Protestant work ethic also described salvation as pre-ordained, but nevertheless endorsed the discipline of work and material success underpinned by prudent, conservative financial management as representing the certainty of one's position among those chosen to be saved. This is what Weeks calls the epistemological reward of work – the knowledge that one would be saved, reflected in one's work. Moreover, Weeks argues that for the Protestant worker in Weber's account, the nature of the task and the financial reward of the work were less relevant than the ethical commitment to work itself, expressed in the effort applied to labour. Working was in this respect a moral duty divorced from the social or material necessity of the task, and from any rewards to be gained in this life. Moreover, the Protestant work ethic reflects a system in which labour takes place under conditions in which the specificity of the working person is irrelevant to the task at hand – conditions that are remote to those described by theorists of immaterial labour, but reflect those of early capitalism.

With the shift to Fordism, Weeks suggests that the promise of the work ethic is transformed from salvation to social mobility – a socio-economic reward. Corresponding with the period between the early twentieth century and the shift to post-Fordism, the Fordist work ethic extended a promise to the industrial working class: work hard and conform to the discipline of the shop floor, and you and your family will be rewarded materially and rise in social status. Again, the Fordist work ethic plays a role in encouraging workers to conform to the disciplinary requirements of labour, only this time the social status offered by work comes to the fore as work's reward. Moreover, the Fordist work ethic takes on this meaning at a time when mass consumption is recognized as critical to sustaining and legitimizing the outputs of mass production. It is the duty of a Fordist worker not only to work, but to spend their wages. In this way, Weeks suggests that in Fordism consumption also emerges as an important economic practice, in contrast to the Protestant work ethic, which opposed work to mere 'idleness'. Indeed, while the Protestant work ethic cautioned against enjoying wealth to the point of failing in one's commitment to work, the continued commitment to work in the Fordist work ethic is underpinned by ceaseless consumption. Production and consumption come together in the Fordist work ethic in a search for the good life offered by the abundance of consumer goods produced through the highly refined systems of Fordist mass production.

The Fordist work ethic maintained a distinction between the subject at work and outside work. The promise of the Fordist work ethic is work hard, and you will be able to enjoy consumption in your non-work time. This distinction dissolves with the post-Fordist work ethic, which arises within economic transformations such as those connected with immaterial labour. Rather than salvation or material reward, the post-Fordist work ethic makes perhaps the greatest promise of all to workers: meaning, fulfilment and self-actualization. As the subjectivity of workers becomes more significant to the nature of work and to the value of labour, Weeks argues that the work ethic has shifted to mandate an ethical commitment to self-realization through work. Here, the reward for work is subjectivity itself, and work becomes a unique and uniquely powerful site for the creation of the self. With an emphasis on self-realization, work also shifts to become a realm of (at least supposed) enjoyment – a position formerly associated only with consumption considered as a separate part of life to work. In the post-Fordist work ethic, the logic of consumption bleeds into the way that subjects are supposed to approach work. With this shift, the post-Fordist work ethic positions the cultivation of the self as an end in itself that is pursued primarily through work, understood as a realm of autonomous self-realization and enjoyment. The post-Fordist work ethic therefore has an ontological reward: the possibility for subjectivity as such, realized in and through the process of becoming a worker. Each transformation in capitalism therefore leads to an intensification of the requirement to invest the self in work:

> With each reconstitution of the work ethic, more is expected of work: from an epistemological reward in the deliverance of certainty, to a socioeconomic reward in the possibility of social mobility, to an ontological reward in the promise of meaning and self-actualization. (Weeks, 2011, p 75)

In general therefore, the work ethic operates as a disciplinary requirement for ethical subject formation that reflects shifts in the social organization of work and the requirements of different kinds of labour, enacted in the relationship between work and the self.

Weeks's work is critical in showing how the mandates of the work ethic have intensified even as unemployment has been repositioned as a necessary and natural part of capitalist societies. Fordist citizenship regimes were built on the 'family wage'. Notions of 'industrial citizenship', such as those explored by Strangleman (2015), theorized how community relationships, family structures and socialization processes were held together through the promise of full employment to male breadwinners. With the shift to post-Fordism, contemporary analyses of citizenship and work have suggested that employment has ceased to become a pathway to substantive citizenship (Turner, 2001), which has itself been eroded by the flexibilization of labour markets. However, Weeks's work is able to situate the new requirements imposed on post-Fordist citizens within the disciplinary requirements of the work ethic to reposition the significance of work for contemporary citizenship. In line with Skeggs's discussion of the self as value (Skeggs, 2011), post-Fordist citizens are required to understand themselves in terms of the accumulation and mobilization of value (seen as being synonymous with subjectivity) in order to cope with welfare arrangements that are marketized and financialized (Adkins, 2017). The post-Fordist work ethic is accompanied by what Jessica Gerrard (2014, p 871) describes as a 'learning ethic', in which notions of lifelong learning capture the contemporary requirement to continually work on the self and accumulate new capacities in order to become economically productive in a rapidly changing labour market. The post-Fordist work ethic therefore describes a mode of citizenship that is organized through the logic of value and enacted through the cultivation of the self as a worker.

Moreover, Weeks suggests that in mandating particular relationships between work and the self, the work ethic has an important role in regulating social class. Weeks argues that the work ethic is a disciplinary discourse designed to produce a compliant labour force that is of use to the valorization strategies employed by capital. The problems of a recalcitrant workforce are front and centre of the Protestant and Fordist eras, in which the work ethic is deployed in order to turn agricultural into industrial workers or to mitigate the upheaval created by struggles between labour and capital during the 1920s, which resulted in the unionized workforces that are now seen as definitive of Fordism. The post-Fordist work ethic is a disciplinary technology for regulating a workforce in which the capacity for self-expression is one of the requirements of contemporary labour, and therefore for regulating the diverse and fragmented workforce of the service economy. However, to conclude this section, I want to suggest that the work ethic's historical relationship with class is more complex and less epochal than Weeks's framework would suggest.

In Weeks's overview of Weber's work and in her discussion of Fordism, the work ethic effectively operates as a way of imposing bourgeois morality on the working class in order to ensure compliance with the demands of industrial labour. However, the post-Fordist work ethic has a more complex classed history than this. For example, as well as exploring the sober self-discipline of the Protestant work ethic, Weber describes middle-class professional labour (such as that performed by the sociologist) in terms of a vocation (Weber et al, 2004) – a term that describes work as a personally significant project with value in itself that is outside either material or spiritual reward. The distinction between vocation and submission to industrial discipline in return for material reward is a clear and long-standing classed distinction that is intrinsic to the Fordist work ethic. Moreover, the notion of vocation anticipates the emphasis on self-actualization that defines the post-Fordist work ethic: while a vocation locates the meaning of work as a socially relevant endeavour rather than as a way of actualizing the self, both see a personal investment in work as a means by which to attribute value to work and to the self. In this respect, even the Fordist work ethic is not homogeneous in its interaction with class, and the post-Fordist work ethic displays both ruptures and continuities with earlier manifestations of the work ethic that are differentiated according to long-standing classed distinctions. Understanding the contemporary work ethic therefore means analysing how its classed history interacts with the emphasis on self-realization that has become critical to post-Fordist working subjectivities – a task taken up in this book.

Youth and the post-Fordist labour force

The movement to post-Fordism and discussions of immaterial labour describe changes in the nature of labour and concordant shifts in the nature and social composition of the labour force that are important contextual factors for understanding the formation of young people as workers. The key shift here is the decline of the figure of the male breadwinner as the touchstone for the social organization of employment, including the mass entry of women into work and the individualization of wages (as opposed to the notion of the family wage of Fordist capitalism). While a focus on the male breadwinner ignores both domestic labour and the long-standing diversity of those engaged in paid work, the post-Fordist labour force is now characterized by the economization of a range of subjectivities beyond the masculine worker of Fordism. One way in which this shift is captured is through the concept of the feminization of work, a phrase that has been used with a variety of meanings in different research traditions, but which in concepts of post-Fordism describes both the mass participation of women in work and changes in the nature of work itself that have made traditionally feminine qualities into desirable attributes of workers in general (Hardt and Negri, 2004). The capacity for empathic communication and reflexive self-presentation is now increasingly demanded of workers across different sectors of the economy, such as consumer services in which interactions constitute the main task of work, and other sectors that require manipulating and communicating information and working in teams. In this respect, the feminization of work has resulted not just in shifts in the gendered composition of the labour force, but in what Lisa Adkins has described as the economization of gender, in which femininity shifts from an attribute of bodies to a quality that circulates to produce value in immaterial economies (Adkins, 2005a; Adkins and Dever, 2016): both men and women are called upon to mobilize what were once considered essentially feminine traits at work, and this requirement produces new inequalities and forms of essentialism as well as more or less deliberate performative practices from workers designed to manipulate these gendered signs (Adkins, 2002).

While the economization of gender is now well recognized in the literature, youth has also shifted into an increasingly significant position within the post-Fordist labour force, although this is not well documented or extensively theorized. The significance of youth to post-Fordism can be approached in similar terms to the feminization of work – that is, in terms of the quantitative increase in young people's participation in work, and in terms of the way that youthful qualities are now considered to be ideal attributes of contemporary workers. In quantitative terms, the significance of youth to particular sectors of the economy is now well documented. Young labour is critical to sectors such as retail and the hospitality industry, including the fast food industry and the broader night-time economy (Tannock, 2001; Besen-Cassino, 2014). Young people are considered ideal workers in these industries because their labour is cheap (owing to legally permitted youth wages below the adult minimum wage) and because they are regarded as flexible workers for whom employment precarity is less of a problem owing to ongoing parental support (Tannock, 2001; Mizen, 2004). In the work of Tannock (2001), fast food chains and large grocery stores actively recruited young people, including students, by promoting themselves as 'fun' employers, which offered young workers the opportunity to socialize and 'goof off' at work while taking advantage of the unserious or stop-gap attitude that most young people adopted towards their work in fast food. The changes in labour force composition described by the feminization of work therefore also include the mass participation of young people in work, which is well recognized as a normative experience for students (Wyn and White, 1997).

Beyond the ubiquity of young people in particular sectors of the economy, youth is an important focal point for governmental interventions designed to produce useful workers. Indeed, in contemporary discourses of youth, the capacity for economic productivity is now essentialized as an attribute of healthy youth development itself. In developmental and neuroscientific approaches to youth development, youth is understood as a time at which young people accumulate the capacity for individualized rationality and emotional maturity. These attributes are increasingly discussed alongside notions of human capital drawn from neoclassical economics, in which youth development underpins the accumulation of human capital and the capacity for its successful exchange on the labour market (Sukarieh and Tannock, 2008; 2014; Farrugia, 2018a). The most evocative example of this can be found in the way that young people are positioned in discussions of global economic development and poverty alleviation, such as in the World Bank development report published in 2007 (World Bank, 2007). In this report, youth is described as a process of social, cognitive and neurological development that is successful to the degree that it supports the accumulation of human capital, and therefore the capacity for young people to become economic agents. Young people with human capital are positioned as critical resources for developing economies, and so young people's decision-making capacities and identities must be carefully monitored, since this will shape 'how human capital is kept safe, developed, and deployed' (World Bank, 2007, p 2). The neurological development of young people underpins the cognitive capacity required to develop human capital and the rational faculties required to deploy it in the marketplace. In this way, the formation of young people as workers takes place through interventions into what are understood as universal developmental processes.

Despite this, young people are also the targets of particularly punitive employment policies, which are designed to address the problem of youth unemployment through interventions into their supposed ethical dispositions towards work. These interventions have a long history, but contemporary approaches reflect the emergence of high levels of youth unemployment as a structural feature of capitalist societies since the 1980s, alongside the emergence of neoliberal employment policies focused essentially on the subjectivities of the unemployed (Griffin, 1993; Mizen, 2004). The basic premise behind these interventions is 'learn or earn', with the threat of benefit sanctions if young people do not engage in some form of sanctioned training or employment. In Australia, where this research was carried out, unemployed young people are now required to perform internships, in which they are paid well below the minimum wage to perform what would otherwise be minimum wage service employment without any prospect of ongoing work. Young people are therefore part of the economization of unemployment through workfare, or the reconfiguring of unemployment as a set of labouring activities designed to produce value for capital (Adkins, 2017).

Beyond interventions into unemployment, a range of mechanisms currently exist that assign a particular value to young people's labour and to young people as workers. The most obvious example of this is the existence of youth wages. Developmental approaches to youth underpin the value that is assigned to young people's labour via youth wages, which in countries such as the United Kingdom and Australia are lower than the minimum wage that applies to adult workers. This is the case regardless of the duties performed, which may be identical to those performed by older workers – a juridical intervention based on the assumption that the value of a worker's labour increases with maturity (Mizen, 2004). This is also the case when the very youthfulness of a worker is important to their value to an employee, such as the examples already discussed in which the flexibility offered by a student workforce supported in part by their parents facilitates employment and labour conditions that may otherwise be challenged by workers (Tannock, 2001). In this sense, youth wages operate as ways both of assigning value to labour and of producing definitions of youth itself – positioning working subjects as 'young' through the employment regimes and labouring practices within which they work.

Aside from these juridical interventions, in post-Fordist or immaterial economies the value associated with young labour goes beyond that captured by wages. Original theorists of immaterial labour positioned youth in terms of a 'pure virtuality' (Lazzarato, 1996, p 135) or an undetermined capacity to produce value in the post-Fordist labour force. However, the insertion of young people into the dynamics of immaterial labour has also made youthfulness itself into a particular kind of value, or a quality that circulates to attribute value to commodities, interactions and subjectivities (Farrugia, 2018b). Young people are popularly associated with up-to-date or cutting-edge cultural consumption and trends, as well as embodying a capacity for carefree enjoyment that resonates with the image cultivated by many brands. As a result, young workers are preferred employees in some service employment because their embodied appearance and modes of self-expression are seen to confer qualities of youthful sophistication and cool onto brands and commodities. The capacity to embody particular kinds of youthfulness is also connected to social class, requiring the right dispositions to recognize and perform youthful cool at work (Farrugia, 2018b). The mobilization and valorization of youthfulness within immaterial economies is an example of the way in which youthful subjectivities are attributed with value within the dynamics of labour and value that make up the post-Fordist economy.

In general therefore, the feminization of work has also included the incorporation of young people into the labour force, and has therefore submitted young people to the disciplinary requirements of labour in a range of significant ways, although these are sometimes contradictory. Youth is a key point of governmental intervention into the labour force. The capacity to produce value represented by notions of human capital is being essentialized into an aspect of healthy youth development, making youth synonymous with the formation of workers. However, the supposed universality of this developmental process is ignored in punitive interventions into youth unemployment, which are designed as much to punish young people for unemployment as to capitalize on the labour they perform as part of workfare programmes specific to youth. Finally, the production and circulation of youthfulness within immaterial economies confers value onto both commodities and youth subjectivities, and thereby repositions youthfulness from an attribute of young people to a product of labour. The post-Fordist work ethic is therefore aligned with the position of young people within post-Fordist work, emphasizing the requirement for young people to cultivate themselves as subjects of value to the labour force. In the next and final substantive part of this section, I sketch an approach to this process – the cultivation of the working self.

The cultivation of the young working self

By focusing on the cultivation of the working self, this book examines how young people respond to shifts in the work ethic, the nature of labour and the position of youth within the contemporary labour force.

A focus on identity construction in its relationship to work resonates in some ways with the notions of individualization and reflexivity that are reviewed in Chapter 1, especially in analysing subjectivity as a way of understanding how young people negotiate structural processes. In particular, the concept of reflexivity draws attention to the relationship of the self to the self, and the significance of work on the self as a response to social change. However, in theories of late modernity, the concept of reflexivity describes a generic attribute of late modern subjects (Farrugia, 2013a) and is used more to understand how young people navigate their biographies in precarious social conditions than to analyse work as a realm for the creation of subjectivity (Farrugia, 2013b). To address this issue, young people's reflexive relationship to themselves must be grounded in the discourses and disciplinary requirements of the post-Fordist work ethic. These requirements are reflected in calls to form the self in line with notions such as employability and other approaches to young working subjects, which I review here as a conceptual backdrop to my approach to young people's personal practices.

Young people are now encouraged to draw on a wide and bewildering array of ideas, resources and practices in engaging with work – a situation that reflects their position as focal points for the creation of the post-Fordist labour force. While the individualization theorists suggest that work has receded in its significance for late modern identities, Angela McRobbie has argued that work is taking on a renewed significance in terms that resonate with the post-Fordist work ethic. Writing about the relationship between work and individualization in the new economy, McRobbie suggests that 'Work has been reinvented to satisfy the needs and demands of a generation who, "disembedded" from traditional attachments to family, kinship, community or region, now find that work must become a fulfilling mark of self' (McRobbie, 2016, p 39).

In other words, as the social structures that underpinned Fordist identities beyond work dissolve, work is repositioned as the critical source of personal fulfilment for contemporary youth. McRobbie argues that 'a desirable job [has become] part of the panoply of attributes through which cultural intelligibility is acquired' (McRobbie, 2016, p 162), precisely as the labour market has become more precarious. In this context, McRobbie suggests that the relationship between subjectivity and work described by theorists of immaterial labour is reflected in discourses of the ideal young worker. In an analysis of social policy discourses deployed to describe young people's position in the new economy, McRobbie finds 'a replacement of skill, expertise and qualifications with the idea of a portfolio which fits into a whole range of wildly different capacities, but also a hugely individualised outlook' (McRobbie, 2016, p 107).

For McRobbie, what counts as an economically valuable dimension of the self has become ambiguous. In this context, the practices that young people are encouraged to use in order to make themselves attractive to employers are becoming increasingly expansive, with a range of agendas targeting youth that draw on the post-Fordist work ethic and on definitions of the working self that are connected with immaterial labour. This can be seen in the emergence of concerns about employability, and the increasingly expansive meaning that this term is acquiring. The notion of employability is used to describe the features of a worker that are likely to be valued by employers, and is part of an individualized discourse in which young people are encouraged to cultivate employability within themselves in order to obtain satisfying work (Sukarieh and Tannock, 2008; Cuzzocrea, 2015). This term is now used both within and outside formal educational institutions, and the spread of calls to employability reflects a bewildering diversity of practices designed to make one employable. These include gap year or volunteer tourism packages that offer feelings of worldliness' and cosmopolitanism (Yoon, 2014), the pressure to acquire educational credentials, the cultivation of personal relationships, and soft skills such as leadership, confidence, personal motivation, self-presentation and teamwork (Cuzzocrea, 2015). Discourses of employability are also critical to the government of youth unemployment and to the way in which inequalities are framed politically. Young unemployed people are approached in terms of their job readiness, and workfare regimes are legitimized in terms of developing employability in young people. The discourse of employability seems to span all areas of a young person's life and all aspects of the labour force. This discourse foregrounds no set of practices in particular, locating productivity in a worker's subjectivity in general rather than in task-specific skills. For this reason, McRobbie (2016) argues that the failure to find pleasure in work constitutes a failure to achieve cultural intelligibility, as if the self is made unviable through a failure to live up to the post-Fordist work ethic.

As notions of employability go beyond the acquisition of skill, young people are also being encouraged (or mandated) to adopt a new relationship with work – that of passionate investment. The notion of passionate labour describes a relationship to work in which a worker enthusiastically invests themselves in work, is successful at work to a degree that is consistent with their level of enthusiasm, and experiences fulfilment and pleasure as a result. While the incitement to passion in work is strongest in the creative and culture industries (McRobbie, 2016), this ethos has spread and now describes a range of forms of labour, as well as welfare interventions into the lives of young people. Analysing the emergence of passion as an ethos that is driving work training programs of unemployed youth, Kelly and

Harrison (2009) describe a governmental regime that requires young workers to demonstrate commitment, autonomy, creativity and pleasure in work in order to successfully participate in training and become workers. In this context, the capacity to mobilize and perform passion is seen to represent an authentic and personally unique investment in work that qualifies young people to receive continued assistance with employment (in this case training as chefs). Passion thereby emerges as a specific way of knowing and producing the self that is consistent with the post-Fordist work ethic, creating questions about the kinds of practices that can produce passionate workers and attribute value to passionate labour.

Addressing this situation, we are at some distance from the social contract view of work, in which workers stand at a distance from the labour market and negotiate it (with varying degrees of reflexivity) on the basis of the resources they possess. The attributes of contemporary employability are not merely resources that a young worker can exchange on the labour market, but rather are inseparable from subjectivity itself, which has become synonymous with the capacity to produce value. Passionate labour is successful not on the basis of skills, but rather on the basis of a young person's personal investment in work, the success of which is reflected in pleasure and self-realization. In both cases, the productive dimensions of the self are no longer alienable from the subject and therefore cannot be successfully exchanged in the labour market relation. The accumulation of resources is therefore not enough to understand the formation of young people as workers. For this reason, there is a need to go beyond existing approaches to reflexivity or employability, which are based on the accumulation or mobilization of resources in exchange for a job. What is needed is a view of subjectivity and of a young person's reflexive relationship to the self that is understood as inseparable from work, and that is therefore in line with the relationship to work mandated by the post-Fordist work ethic.

In this book, I approach the formation of the young working self in terms of the ethical relationship that young people adopt towards work. In this, my analysis is guided by the concept of the post-Fordist work ethic, as well as by the need to differentiate young people's relationship to the precepts of the work ethic in relation to social class, and to understand the work ethic as productive of a diverse range of subject positions. The work of Foucault and Bourdieu both offer theoretical sensibilities to guide my analysis of the work ethic. While they come from different theoretical traditions, these two authors share a concern with the reflexive and contextual use of theoretical concepts to understand the relationship between subjectivity and power, offering not strict overarching frameworks but instead flexible tools to understand and critique social arrangements (Ball, 2006). They offer a view of the formation of young people as workers that situates the post-Fordist work ethic as a disciplinary framework and technology of the self, which is taken up differently by young people occupying different positions within post-Fordist economies of value and the self.

In some ways, the post-Fordist work ethic is similar to what Foucault would describe as a technology of the self (Foucault, 1988), through which young people create a relationship to the self and to others through the formation of themselves as workers. For Foucault, technologies of the self are practices or techniques through which subjectivities are constituted within the terms offered by available discourses. The key difference between reflexivity and Foucauldian techniques is that the latter are embedded within and articulate power relationships at the level of subjectivity and the body, and therefore do not describe the actions of a self-aware subject but one whose self-awareness is made available by the disciplinary requirements within which they are embedded. As a technology of the self, the post-Fordist work ethic mandates the cultivation of the self in line with an ethical commitment to being productive, and to producing a self that offers value to employers and to the labour force. Approaching the post-Fordist work ethic as a technology of the self means situating a reflexive relationship to the self not as a response to precarity but as a disciplinary requirement for subject formation that is specific to work. In this sense, reflexive self-examination is a means by which the post-Fordist work ethic is articulated on the level of actual lived subjectivities in their most intimate dimensions. This means that rather than the relationship of a subject who stands at a distance from the labour market and negotiates it reflexively, as critiqued in Chapter 1, this is a reflexive relationship to the self that reflects the ethical mandates and disciplinary requirements of contemporary work.

This focus on embodied practices is also shared by Bourdieu, whose emphasis on the relationship between class and value was foreshadowed in Chapter 1, and whose theory of practice emphasizes how classed dispositions shape practices and orientations to cultural distinctions. For Bourdieu (1990), the self is formed through a practical engagement with social structures, which produces a relatively enduring set of dispositions. These dispositions amount to a 'habitus', which is embodied and not available for conscious reflection. Dispositions guide practices, these being regularized improvisations produced through an interaction between the habitus and the structural conditions that differently positioned groups confront, and are oriented towards accumulating symbolic value. Class inequalities shape practices via the dispositions of the habitus, which reflects the structural conditions of its production. Class distinction is one key example of this, in which those with large stocks of cultural capital cultivate tastes that are considered refined or prestigious. Bourdieu (1984, pp 53–56) describes this in terms of a 'distance from necessity', in which middle-class dispositions are opposed to crass materialism or modes of consumption oriented towards material gratification, and are thereby positioned as elevated or transcendent. In this way, dispositions shaped by objective distance from material necessity shape practices oriented towards reproducing and valorizing this distance in the symbolic world. Distinction is a model for practice in general, in which classed dispositions provide guiding orientations for creative practices aimed at accumulating value and attributing value to the self.

Bourdieu's concept of the habitus also represents an approach to the embodiment of history, or the way in which long-standing collective responses to structural inequality are embodied and thereby continue to shape practices in new social environments. This aspect of Bourdieu's work is useful for situating contemporary identities within the classed history of the work ethic. As discussed earlier, the post-Fordist work ethic has operated as a means for disciplining the industrial and post-Fordist working class while promoting forms of self-realization anticipated by professional vocations. There are therefore questions about how classed identities contribute to the nature of the post-Fordist work ethic that relate to the relationship between distinction, subjectivity and work. What is the relationship between young people's ethical relationship with work and social class, including processes of class distinction? How does this relationship play out in the way that young people understand themselves as productive subjects and in their definitions of meaningful work? How does class shape the aspirations for self-realization through work that are so critical to the post-Fordist work ethic? These questions are explored throughout this book by situating the post-Fordist work ethic as a means by which contemporary classed subjectivities are produced. This is approached in terms of the cultivation of the self as a subject of value – not merely symbolic value in general, but specifically in relation to the requirements of the contemporary labour force.

In general, therefore, this book approaches youth subjectivities in terms of how the post-Fordist work ethic is taken up and articulated in the cultivation of the self as a subject of value to the workforce. My approach here is consistent with the broader emphasis on reflexivity as an attribute of contemporary subjectivities to be found in theories of late modernity, but is aimed at overcoming conceptual problems specific to the relationship between youth and work in post-Fordism. These include the social contract view of work that drives the concept of youth transitions, as well as the increasingly intense pressure that young people face to construct themselves as productive subjects that will be seen as valuable in the post-Fordist labour market, including the cultivation of personal attributes rather than task-specific skills. This is understood as a process of constitution parallel to that of Foucault, in which subjects are formed within the disciplinary requirements of post-Fordist work, and are then actively taken up and deployed in the projects of self-realization mandated by the post-Fordist work ethic. The relationship between class and the way that the work ethic is articulated is understood through the work of Bourdieu, situating the formation of the working self as a realm for the practice of classed distinction. In this way, my aim is to understand how notions of value and productivity are actively taken up and used in the formation of classed subjects through the cultivation of the working self.

Conclusion

My aim in this chapter has been to substantiate and theorize the main focus of this book – youth, work and the post-Fordist self. In particular, I have focused on the changing relationship between subjectivity and work described by theories of post-Fordism and immaterial labour. These concepts describe changes in the social organization and biopolitics of work that situate subjectivity in its most general sense as a process of value creation. These shifts require new ways of understanding the formation of the working self – a process that I address here through the notion of the post-Fordist work ethic. The work ethic is a disciplinary technology that mandates an ethical commitment to work as the basis for subjectivity in capitalism. The nature of this commitment has changed over time, but in post-Fordism the work ethic has expanded beyond distinctions between work and the rest of social life to promise self-actualization in the most expansive sense as the reward for a personal investment in work. There are good reasons to believe that young people are at the forefront of the post-Fordist work ethic, as exemplified by the incitements to employability and passionate labour that are targeted at the relationship young people adopt towards work. Consistent with the post-Fordist work ethic, these terms encourage young people to cultivate a variety of personal attributes in the formation of themselves as workers, and to invest the entirety of their affective lives in their work. For this reason, the formation of young people as workers means the constitution of the self as a subject of the post-Fordist work ethic through the cultivation of the self as a subject of value to the labour force.

In the process, I have raised a number of issues connected to the specific practices through which post-Fordist selves are produced, and how these practices contribute to inequality and difference among the youth labour force, such as those connected with social class. The remainder of this book addresses these questions, and empirically examines the practices and ethics that young people draw upon in the cultivation of themselves as workers. In the process, the book examines the way in which differently positioned young people understand themselves as productive subjects, and explores what self-realization actually means for young people from different class backgrounds and with different aspirations and experiences of work. By deploying the post-Fordist work ethic empirically, the book subjects some of the claims made by theories of post-Fordism and the post-Fordist work ethic to scrutiny. In particular, the book reveals new dynamics of post-Fordist subject formation that are unrecognized in these existing theories and relate to the contemporary dynamics of social class. Issues such as the dissolution between the production and unproductive dimensions of the self, the investment of one's whole self in work and the alignment between self-realization and economic productivity offer a new focus for studies of youth and work, but offer little insight into the actually existing practices through which young people form themselves as workers. Examining these practices will reveal how the classed history of the work ethic is played out in the post-Fordist present through the practices of distinction and self-cultivation that are critical to the formation of classed subjectivities among young people. The first empirical chapter of this book describes those young people whose identities as workers most closely resemble the post-Fordist ideal: middle-class 'subjects of passion' for whom the entirety of the self is folded into an affective investment in productivity and in work.

3

Passionate Subjects and the Middle-Class Self at Work

This is the first of three empirical chapters exploring the ethics and practices through which young people are formed as workers. In this and the chapters that follow, I will use the concept of the post-Fordist work ethic to examine young people's narratives about the meaning of work, the way they understood their value to the labour market and to employers, and the way they cultivated working selves. My aim here is to foreground the ethical commitments and self-definitions that intertwine in the way that young people articulate the post-Fordist work ethic in relation to themselves, and to analyse how young people position themselves as ethical subjects within the dictates of the work ethic. Through a focus on the relationship between definitions of productivity and subjectivity in general, these chapters are also aimed at applying empirical scrutiny to some of the claims made in theories of post-Fordism and in the narrative about the relationship between class and the work ethic described in Chapter 2. In particular, this chapter and the next explore distinctions between the Fordist promise of social mobility and the post-Fordist offer of self-realization through work. In the process, this chapter – and the book in general – also examine the suggestion that distinctions between the productive and unproductive dimensions of the self are no longer useful for understanding the relationship between subjectivity and work because the entirety of the self has become subsumed into work. These arguments provide the guiding orientation to the analyses that follow, which focus on how young people understand the productive dimensions of their identities and what ethical relationship they adopt towards work. By focusing on young people's narratives, the remainder of this book will argue that the post-Fordist work ethic has become part of the way in which classed subjectivities are formed, and will therefore show how different relationships between productivity, value and the self contribute to classed subjectivities in post-Fordism.

As is reflected in its title, in this chapter I will describe what I am calling 'passionate subjects', a term that describes what I will suggest is an intermingling of classed distinction (Bourdieu, 1990) and the post-Fordist work ethic's promise of self-realization through a total investment in work. In his theorization of distinction, Bourdieu (1984) describes class privilege in terms of the ascription of prestige to powerful social groups, such that their value is understood as essential to their being rather than to anything in particular that they have achieved. This mode of distinction is actualized in the narratives of subjects of passion, although this takes a specific form as a manifestation of the post-Fordist work ethic. Passionate subjects come from middle-class backgrounds with family histories of tertiary education and professional employment. Passionate subjects relate to work through an ethic of passion, a term that describes a total personal and affective investment in work as a realm that realizes the intrinsic creative energies of the self in its most general sense. A subject of passion becomes productive by mobilizing their intrinsically passionate nature in the cultivation of themselves as workers, but in order to be successful at work passionate subjects must nurture passion in everything they do. Work is therefore described as a realm that is not distinct from any other part of a subject's life, being approached through cultivating a passionate life in general, both within and outside the realm of work. In the process, passionate subjects frequently describe their work in terms of a desire to make a 'positive difference' in the lives of others, even when their aspirations or actual employment experiences are not in fields, such as the non-governmental organization (NGO) sector or the helping professions, that are typically understood in this way. Passionate work therefore enlarges the significance of work beyond personal self-interest and is described as a form of self-realization that is not associated with mere material necessity. In this sense, passionate subjects describe work in terms of a distance from necessity, which intermingles traditional modes of middle-class distinction with the self-realization intrinsic to the post-Fordist work ethic.

Passion as an ethic of self-realization

Many young people in this book were anxious about the prospect of being in work that they did not enjoy or that did not reflect their identity in some way. However, the relationship between work and the self varied in significant ways – both in terms of the definition of the working self and the relationship between identity, productivity and the experience of work, which together make up the ethic through which young people are formed as workers. Young people who relate to work through an ethic of passion come closest to the ideal subject of the post-Fordist work ethic, in which the whole of the self is invested in and realized through work. For passionate subjects, a total investment in work is considered the ideal relationship between work and the self, and the expansion of work into other aspects of life is described as desirable for a satisfying life in the most general sense. Distinctions between the self inside and outside work are seen to reflect a dissatisfaction with work and a failure for the working subject to appropriately cultivate a satisfying working life. This was articulated by passionate subjects across a range of age groups and working situations, including the following narrative from Beth, a young woman interviewed in her final year of high school at age 18:

> 'I don't understand why you'd do a job where you have to change who you were for … I don't think people should have to be a different person at their job and then come home and they're a different person. If their job changes them, that's all right, because they're choosing to change it. But if they let the job change them and they don't want it, then that's where the problem starts.
>
> 'I don't just want a job where I'm at work, I do it and then I come home and it's whatever. I want a job where I'm passionate about it. I want a job where I come home and I still want to be working, like it's something that I feel passionate about and I'm like, oh, I really want to do this now. I don't want something like, oh, thank God the day's over. I want to do something where the day finishes, I'm like, oh my God, like I'll have to keep doing this when I get home.
>
> 'I just think why would you spend your whole life doing something you don't like? I know that's what everyone does because it's money, but I'm just like, you have the choice. Why wouldn't you pick to do something you love? Even if it's something you're not making as much money on, I'm sure if you love it enough, you could find a way to make it work.'

Framed in aspirational terms, this narrative begins with a desire for coherence in the self across work and the rest of social life, positioning work as a realm for the authentic expression of the passionate self. Ideally, work does not require a worker to be a 'different person at their job', but rather offers a kind of autonomous self-realization in which working subjects can choose forms of work that they are passionate about –

an act of individual agency that is driven by the intrinsic passions of a worker and that realizes these passions in work. This young person aspires to an idealized form of passionate work, in which the irresistible attraction of work comprises a unique form of pleasure and fulfilment that the passionate subject welcomes as definitive of life in general. The realization of passion here is seen as a more important aspiration than the accumulation of wealth, and in fact passion is understood as significant enough that it offers a 'way to make it work' in the face of adversity. Something similar was described by Meg, a young tertiary-educated woman who was working as a junior accountant when I first interviewed her:

> 'I don't really see work as a separate part of my life. I just want to have one whole life and I want to be able to do the things I want to do. But I absolutely know that I have to be passionate about everything I do, or I'm not going to do it ... I can't be vibrant about things – like when I think about things that I'm not passionate about I feel dull ... I think I can bring passion to almost anything ... I think I'm really just a passionate person but there are definitely things that excite me more than other things.'

Like other passionate subjects, Meg stressed that work was not a separate part of life, but rather a realm among others that expresses and allows the cultivation of passion. Passionate subjects are therefore realized across the whole of life, positioning work as an extension of a life of passionate investment. Moreover, this narrative introduces the complex nature of passion itself as both a force that an intrinsically passionate person brings to their life and their work, but also as a feeling of personal excitement that is elicited when a subject comes into contact with their passion. Passion in this sense is seen as a kind of affect, both an attribute of the passionate subject and an experience that is made possible when a passionate person becomes excited by things they feel passionately towards. The success or otherwise of passionate investments for this participant is reflected in affective experiences and embodied feelings: the feeling of being 'vibrant about things' as opposed to feeling 'dull' when thinking about things that do not excite passion. The aim of work is therefore not merely career progression or financial reward, but the feeling of vibrance that comes from the actualization of the passionate self at work.

For middle-class passionate subjects, success at work is described in terms of the cultivation of the self – personal growth and self-realization across the whole of life both inside and outside work. Importantly, passionate subjects consistently focused on personal development as the key measure of success and positioned personal development both as a requirement for successful work and the ultimate aim of working itself. Specific achievements such as status, promotion or financial remuneration were either absent from their narratives or were discussed in oblique terms, as in the following quote from Peter, a young man who had recently secured a junior position as an engineer:

> 'Any form of success would be just to be able to grow. I'm not too like – the amount isn't ... Whether it's all over the top and that, it doesn't faze me, but I just want to be able to grow.'
> 'So for you success is just growing yourself as a person?'
> 'Yeah ... what I'm doing professionally ... does apply personally as well ... personally I do want to succeed, professionally as well. So they're not separate.'

In this narrative, financial remuneration is raised and then immediately glossed as unimportant, although as a tertiary-educated young man who has managed to obtain professional employment this participant can be reasonably confident in his future earning potential. Instead, it is personal growth that is the key marker of success in work. Passion is also required for success, becoming both the basis and the outcome of passionate work. This was articulated by the following two participants, including Alice, a young woman in the final year of high school:

> 'You've got – you know you don't just go to work and you've got your work face and then come home and then you've got your home face. You're just the same person ... If it's going to be successful you have to be passionate about it.'

Here, the coherence of the self across work and the rest of life is seen as the basis for the passion of working subjects whose success is driven by their intrinsically passionate nature. Adrian – a junior accountant – was interviewed just after having applied for and achieved a sideways movement to a new role within his firm, which he considered to be a step forward in a successful career:

> 'I think it is my quest for personal development ... That was a contributing factor to my success in this role. It was that you have so much energy, so much drive and so much ambition to develop yourself outside of your career, we think you are the person that is suited to this dynamic role ... It was all of

my other pursuits that has led to me being such a busy person that got it across the line. So definitely my personal journey is one that maintains my intrinsic energy levels I think and that continues to furnish my passion and continues to, I guess, re-evaluate my direction and re-evaluate my passion.'

In this narrative, Adrian attributes his success to his passion, which he emphasizes throughout the interview is not specific to work, but can be seen across a range of pursuits. These included his role in a local sporting team, in which he organizes sport and social events, his position within his social circle, in which he says he facilitates relationships and takes the lead organizing gatherings, and in a broader community involvement in which he volunteers for charity organizations and runs a local organization for young professionals. These, he suggests, reflect his passion, drive and commitment to personal development that have facilitated his success both inside and outside work. In this sense, passion is its own reward, the basis for success and a signifier of self-realization through work.

As well as facilitating career success, passion is also the ethic through which passionate workers navigate their way through the labour market. This is because passion is understood as an affective force that is specific to the subject, rather than to any job or life situation in particular. Since what counts is passion, then the capacity to be passionate or to make a passionate commitment is seen to guide young people through a precarious and contingent labour market. This was articulated both by young people still in education and by older participants with a more substantial experience of professional life. Mary, a student in the final year of high school, expressed the significance of passion as an ethic through which the labour market can be negotiated:

'I always believe that even if it's something you don't like if you try really hard to succeed in that you'll succeed in other areas of your life. So that passion and that drive that you take in one job will follow with you through to another.'

In this narrative, passion and drive will follow the passionate worker regardless of the particular job, and this participant even described herself as passionate about her casual employment in a fast food chain, opposing herself to others who were there merely for the wage. Alex was 30 years old at the time of the interview and working in human relations. Throughout the interview, he returned a number of times to the phrase 'passion spins the plot', an expression that he used to describe the significance of passionate investment as a driving force throughout his working life. Asked about his particular goals or milestones of success, his response intertwines the notion of passion as a driving force for labour market engagement and the notion of passionate self-realization as the ultimate end goal of work, divorced from any particular material signifier of success:

> 'I daresay that I'm more inclined to focus on relationships and let destiny take over a little. I think I'd be – my personality, I'd limit myself if I had a very direct goal and was just focused on that. Long term, do I have goals now? Yeah, of course. Do I have life goals? Sure. Work goals, if I'm enjoying what I'm doing, that's what's important. I'm enjoying what I'm doing now.'

Here, passion is described as an affect that is unique to his personality, but also as a kind of semi-autonomous force guiding passionate workers towards their destiny. At this point it is hard not to recall the original work of Weber on the vocation, or the career (such as that of the politician or the sociologist) that operates as a calling to which the worker responds. There is a sense here that passion operates in a similar way, as a process of self-realization that a worker is fated to experience so long as they allow this passionate force to 'take over a little'. However, Weber's original discussion of work as a calling or a vocation retains a sense of asceticism and personal sacrifice, and the pursuit of aims that go beyond personal satisfaction, such as scientific reason (Weber et al, 2004). For Weber, vocations often take place in precarious and contingent conditions (such as the academy even of Weber's Germany), which the worker suffers through for the sake of this higher aim. Vocations are deliberately remote from the pursuit of happiness and do not foreground enjoyment as a justification for the work. Therefore, while the ethic of passion described in this book retains the emphasis on personal commitment and passionate investment in work, asceticism and self-sacrifice is replaced with the search for personal fulfilment and self-realization. In this sense, the notion of passion as destiny reaches back to the long-standing classed history of the work ethic, in which the middle-class professions offer forms of self-realization that go beyond material success, but transformed in the post-Fordist present to place the development of the self as the aim of passionate labours.

For Alex, as for passionate subjects in general, the capacity to produce value and to be productive at work comes from their passion and from leading a passionate life in a general sense. Their value to employers was therefore described in terms of their capacity to realize and express an authentic self at work. This included a participant's entire personality and enrolled their capacity for self-expression into their understanding of themselves as a subject of value to the labour force. Asked about what he attributed his success at work to, this participant foregrounded his capacity for authentic self-expression:

> 'I am who I am. I'm outgoing, I'm social. I find myself in those situations where other people necessarily won't, because of my personality. But it's confidence and maturity in that I know I'm appropriate. I know I'm genuine. I know I'm communicating a message of this is who I am. So I'm feeling confident in that. I'm confident in dealing with whoever ... I believe if you're lucky enough to be a position of work that reflects your personality or you can reflect your personality through, then you should be proud of it.'

For Alex, it was the authenticity of the self-expression that he found in his work that facilitated his success and underpinned the enjoyment and pride that he gained from work. Having an authentic relationship between work and the self is therefore a necessary condition for passionate self-realization, which in turn is understood as synonymous with productivity and value creation. Moreover, because work is a realm of authentic self-expression, passionate workers see themselves as creating value through their passionate commitment, rather than through any particular skill or personal capacity.

In his most widely cited work on culture and inequality, Bourdieu describes distinctions between those who are seen in terms of what they do and those whose value is seen merely in terms of who they are, and whose 'being' is therefore irreducible to any 'doing' (Bourdieu, 1984, p 23). This form of distinction can be seen in the narratives of subjects of passion, who consider their value to be expressed merely in the cultivation of themselves, rather than in any particularly skilful working practice. It is passion and self-actualization rather than being 'good at' anything in particular that constitutes them as subjects of value to the labour force. For this reason, passionate subjects did not focus on the accumulation of skills in preparation for work, meaning that educational credentials were not a significant part of their narratives despite all being either tertiary educated or in the process of gaining a degree. Instead, it was their passionate commitment to work and to themselves that acted as qualifications for a valued place in the labour force. Moreover, because passion is intrinsic to them as passionate workers, the value that passionate subjects produce is not limited to work, but rather the value of the working self is also realized in other domains of life. Adrian exemplified this:

> 'I have this ambition to become a thought leader. I'd really like to be – and whether that's in a professional sense in my career, whether it's in extracurricular, or whether it's like at home or in sport, that's what I'd like to get to, that's my utopia … I feel that I could be a thought leader across all of those domains and it's just a matter of finding what value I can add to each of those particular areas.'

In this narrative, Adrian's ambition was to find 'what value I can add' to a range of domains in his life, including but not limited to his work. Here, the creation of value shifts beyond the realm of work or the economy, and becomes an ethic through which this participant relates to life in a more general sense, that is as a practice of value creation in multiple interconnected domains. His ambition is represented by the figure of the 'thought leader', who possesses no particular knowledge but who nevertheless contributes value across his life through the passion and authenticity of his commitments and through the cultivation of the self. This is a significant aspect of what makes the work of the passionate subject more than merely a job:

> 'I want a job that's not just a job, that's going to make a difference, has a purpose.'

An insistence on the broader significance of work as a passionate project that 'makes a difference' was common throughout passionate subjects' narratives, and intertwined personal satisfaction and enjoyment with the feeling of having performed work that was socially worthwhile and 'made a difference' in the world:

> 'Yeah and I want to – at the end of the day I want to do a job that makes me feel good about myself, that I've actually done something for someone.'

Here, the value produced by a worker spills out into the whole of life, enlarging the significance of the self so that the cultivation of the self 'makes a difference' to others. The capacity to produce value is therefore not merely an aspect of the working self. Instead, the dissolution of the boundary between the self as worker and the remainder of life means that the logic of value becomes a way in which passionate workers make sense of life in general, and a way that the significance of the self is elevated beyond the material rewards of work (represented by the notion of the job). Understood as a form of class distinction, the ethic of passion therefore reflects aspects of what Bourdieu (1990) describes as the principle of *noblesse oblige*, or the obligation of the nobility to behave with generosity towards others. In this instance, this sense of obligation becomes part of the post-Fordist work ethic through the capacity to produce value across the whole of life, and is explored in more detail in the next section of this chapter.

Cosmopolitanism and work as an ethical project

For passionate subjects, the successful actualization of a passionate working self was described not merely in terms of a passionate and authentic working life, but also manifested in a broader ethical commitment to work as socially significant and as having a positive impact on the lives of others. This was the case for young people of a range of ages and with a diverse range of educational and labour market experience, including those who worked in professions traditionally associated with helping others and those (such as the junior accountants discussed earlier) whose work is not usually associated with an altruistic commitment to the common good. However, what becomes clear throughout these narratives is that the notion of making a difference operates here as a form of class distinction, or a sort of *noblesse oblige* in which supporting others is synonymous with realizing one's essential value and maintaining distinctions between the self and less distinguished others. This process of attributing value to the self through the idea (if not the actuality) of helping others is critical to the ethic of passion. As Renea described, passion can be reflected in a varied and challenging work environment and in work that allows advocacy or minority groups:

> 'I'm very passionate. Like I've always been passionate about advocacy for minority groups. Like I did it through high school and things. So I just really want a job where I can be very active and – I don't know, in that it has a challenge, and I love being challenged. I just – I guess I'd like to be in a working environment where every day is something different.'

Whereas for Julia, who was studying at university, passion and the social significance of work was reflected in a broader awareness of 'wider political circumstances', which in her case included environmental destruction and poverty:

> 'But like I do – I try to surround myself by people that are aware of things. Maybe not necessarily – I only just surround myself by confronting people, but just people that are aware of wider political circumstances.
>
> 'I mean I think any job that people are in – especially if it's a job where power or influence comes in, it's important for people to be really aware of their power and their influence and be passionate about it.'

For Julia, the significance of work was part of a broader reflexive awareness about power and privilege, and her ideal working life was one in which she was surrounded by others who shared her passion for social justice. Positioning the significance of work beyond the individual or material reward is critical to the kind of relationship with work that passionate subjects are cultivating, and also forms the basis for the distinction between passionate work and a mere job, Alex said of his time working in the welfare sector:

> 'Whilst I've had to look for that passion a few times, it's been pretty constant. Really liked the human side of it and helping people with genuine barriers to employment, overcome them, and stand on their own two feet or be proud and change their life kept me turning up every day ... I don't want a "job".'

In this respect, passion and an ethical commitment to work that makes a difference is also a form of distinction in which work takes on a significance beyond material compensation, although typically by young people who are working in or towards well-remunerated professional work. Work that makes a difference is a means by which the value of the self can be realized by passionate subjects beyond their own particular jobs, while also bringing satisfaction to the passionate self. For Adrian, a professional identity also included contributing to charities or foundations at an executive level:

> 'My aspirations are to lead a multinational organization ... I would like to be on the board of a charity or a foundation that has national reach.'

What matters most here is the scale of the organization he is contributing to, rather than the particular issue that his work addresses. This aligns with the ethic of passion through which these young people are formed as workers, in which passion is not specific to any particular realm of existence, but is rather a kind of affective force or energy that a subject brings with them to create value across the whole of life. For this reason, the aspiration to make a difference is not confined to any particular social issue, but rather seen as a general capacity to produce value in the lives of others. However, as the recent university graduate Kate said, this process also contributes to the rewards of passionate labours for the worker themselves:

> 'I'd rather be doing something where I am uplifted and inspired, rather than something where I'm like, oh that's right, this is why humanity sucks ... Yeah, and that's something that I've felt very strongly about since I was young. I don't want to be in a job that I hate. I don't want to be just getting by and making money because that's what people do. If it means that I have to struggle a little bit financially – but be doing something that I feel very passionately about and that I'm getting a lot out of personally – I'd rather be doing that.'

For Kate, the aspiration is for work that makes her feel 'inspired', or that realizes the creative energies of her passionate commitments. This recalls the narrative from Meg, describing work that makes the worker feel 'vibrant' as opposed to 'dull'. Here, work that makes the worker feel inspired (or vibrant) is opposed to 'just getting by and making money', and connected with an ethical commitment to work that connects the worker with the best aspects of humanity. In this sense, the desire to feel inspired and to make a difference is key to the distinction between a job and the work of the passionate subject, which ideally has a broad significance and a positive impact in line with the ideals of the worker. As Kate went on to discuss, 'just getting by and making money' describes not merely those who work in poorly remunerated and less satisfying jobs than herself, but rather those who may be financially well off but are motivated by materialistic concerns such as home ownership, or the aspirations of previous generations, including her parents. Philippa and Megan articulated this when they were interviewed together:

Philippa: 'Well, I think that some of our friends ... they have mortgages and they have partners ... they're doing renovations on their houses, they've like done all their stuff ... but then I've got all these life experiences that they don't have.'

Megan:	'The house, their family, a nice life … if that's what makes you happy that's fine. I would rather travel and use my privilege in life, like not being born in the Gaza Strip or something, to help others. I actually don't care about, yeah, I don't like money.'
Philippa:	'Like I think that there's so much difference between generations, like inter-generation differences now are so vast. Like our parents had houses, got married young, I guess, of that generation, but now we will often change jobs several times in our lives, we may never own a house, we can get job experiences in many different careers, I guess, so I don't know if it's that important to me. Like there's goals I want to achieve in life. I'd like to help educate others so that they're not that ignorant to world issues … and I think climate change as well are the biggest issues facing our planet, so I'd like to raise awareness about that as well.'

In this narrative, the significance of 'world issues' is counterposed to a life primarily focused on conventional aspirations reflecting what Beck would call first modernity – marriage, home ownership and a steady career in a single industry or for a single employer. Instead of this more conventional and – in the mind of this young woman – rather insulated and selfish pathway, her passionate work (as a lawyer) offers the opportunity to connect with issues of global significance. Indeed, framing work in cosmopolitan terms – that is, as an exercise in thinking globally – was a common way in which the significance of work was elevated beyond material necessity. This reflects the broader role that notions of cosmopolitanism have come to play in the practice of middle-class distinction in the wealthy economies of the global north, in which the cultivation of global dispositions is considered part of a well-rounded graduate CV, reflecting employability and 'polish' (Farrugia, 2018a). Melinda was applying to universities when I interviewed her, and for her the practice of class distinction through work that makes a difference was also articulated on the stage of the global:

'I grew up in a great area, I had every opportunity in the world, yeah, it's a nice place, and it's beautiful, like I lived on the beach and all that sort of thing too. I guess it's just small, for me. It's too small for what I want to do and where I want to go.

'This is just my experience, and I can't say that it's the same for everyone, but I'm in an upper middle- to upper-class white society that everything is the same, everyone does the same things, and it just kind of doesn't appeal to me at all. Yeah, and I also like, it sounds cheesy, but I would like to have a job where I do make a genuine difference.'

'What kind of genuine difference?'

'I don't know, whether it's working for an NGO in the Middle East, or Africa, or like policymaking, that sort of thing, to the masses, I guess, yeah.'

This narrative reflects long-standing distinctions between Western cosmopolitans and those in the formerly colonized 'elsewhere' in need of assistance (Sheppard and Leitner, 2010), which have become key to the way that cosmopolitan citizenship is understood by young people in privileged locations in the global north (Farrugia, 2018a). These narratives also resonate with the work of Allen and Hollingworth (2013), who describe distinctions between 'sticky subjects' and 'cosmopolitan creatives', in which the middle-class habitus is articulated through aspirations for mobility and the capacity for producing value through creativity in the global economy. In both cases, the desire to act with significance on a global scale is articulated primarily in relation to work, in which narratives about work become a way that the value of the self is enlarged beyond the immediate local or professional context.

Alongside these cosmopolitans, other passionate subjects across both research sites described their ethical relationship to work in terms of an investment in their local communities. For these young people, the value of themselves and their passionate commitments was actualized in the changes they were able to make within their immediate local areas, which they characterized as part of a process of local economic development. Maxine worked in marketing, and described a passionate commitment to 'seeing things come to life' in her local area:

> 'But the things that always remain constant in the work that I do is that it has to be either community orientated, have a cultural aspect to it or be creative in some way...and that I'm really passionate about – yeah, seeing things come to life [here] ... So yeah, I guess I'm kind of known and I do a lot of networking and attend a lot of events. I do try and help people as much as I can with all those types of things.'

Here, her work contributes to the cultural development of her city, which (as discussed in Chapter 1) has a history of industrial labour and is traditionally seen as a working-class area, a perception that the local government is trying to shift. In this sense, her commitment to helping others with creative events situates her work as part of a broader political and cultural shift taking place in the city, in which older working-class forms of industrial labour make way for a new creative economy (cf Allen and Hollingworth, 2013). Peter was part of a young professionals association in the rural city, and positioned his work as part of a broader process of economic and cultural development in which his locality was made more 'progressive':

'So the young professionals are basically just, in essence, a networking group. I want to try to make it lean a bit more towards connecting like the young people in [this town] Not so much the new people but all the existing people. I find a lot of people are moving in and starting up businesses, taking up management positions [here], which is really I guess going to be a bit more excited about the town. Well it shows we've got a bit more of a future now and I want to be able to make a way for us to actually get together, use the power of numbers to actually have an influence on the town ... Make it a bit more progressive.'

For Peter, the creation of an association for young people based primarily on their status as middle-class professionals is described as an effort to create a future for the community that is based on new businesses and the growth of professional employment. This takes place not merely on the basis of the actual work performed but rather through the presence of energetic and passionate young people in the community. This was also articulated by Adrian:

'I feel like I have a lot to offer [this place] in terms of my energy ... I feel that even by being a part of the city I'm actively contributing to its change process. That to me is quite valuable ... I'd ultimately like to see [this place] as a destination city. By that I mean not only destinations for tourists but a destination for professionals. I would like to see [us] become home to a number of head offices whereby young professionals and experienced executives can remain here, embrace the ... lifestyle whilst getting the challenges of that higher level.'

Like the notion of passion in general, here it is the personal affective forces brought to bear on the local community that contribute to the development of the city, rather than Adrian's labour as such. In general, therefore, passionate workers see themselves as making valuable contributions towards social and political issues beyond their own individual lives through their existence as passionate subjects and through the outpouring of their energies throughout their social commitments. This is the case for both passionate cosmopolitans and locally invested participants, both of whom understand their energies as contributing to positive and progressive social change. This is manifested in economic development that either alleviates global poverty or changes the cultural image and economic fabric of their local community. In either case, what is critical from the perspective of the passionate worker is that their value is realized not merely in their own lives, but rather in their social and cultural environment as well. Of course, this is also aligned with realizing the value of themselves, and the two are regarded as synonymous, as Meg's response to an answer about her ambitions and plans for the future shows:

> 'Everything's always changing and I have the big picture, which is I want to be my best self and I want to help people and contribute to the community. That's kind of the overarching goal.'

For this young woman, becoming her best self, helping others and contributing to her local community intertwine into a broader project of personal development and value creation, in which the attribution of value to the self is also the creation of value for others. This young woman goes on to say that this is not a deliberate or strategic process, but an authentic expression of herself and her own energy for supporting others through her work as an accountant:

> 'I don't like saying it's strategic. I just think I want to be an accountant and a consultant because I genuinely want to help people and I think if I come across someone or something where I think I can help, I'll put it forward. It's not I just want to win any client that will come to me.'

To summarize my argument thus far, passion operates for these young people as an ethic for the formation of the self as a worker and is a means by which class distinction is achieved within the post-Fordist work ethic. Passion is understood as an affect that is unique to the self and drives a project of personal self-actualization, which is realized in the ongoing outpouring of passionate investment. Passion is not a particular skill and relates to no aspect of the subject in particular. Instead, what matters is that the passionate subject brings passion to the whole of their life, and then develops this passion inside and outside work. Moreover, passion is the source of value both in the self and in work, and is realized in every aspect of the passionate subject's life. The value of the passionate subject is realized most clearly and effectively at work, but can also be seen in the value that passionate workers bring to others through their ethical commitments. Across the board, passion is a means by which the significance of work is positioned beyond material necessity, and therefore aligns with the process of class distinction initially theorized by Bourdieu, but this time specifically in the process of the formation of the self as a worker. Passion is therefore synonymous with the creation of value and the attribution of the value to work, others and the self. In what remains of this chapter, I explore the final aspect of the formation of the passionate self, focusing on the practices that young people foreground in the cultivation of themselves as subjects of value.

Cultivating the passionate subject: passion as the whole of life

The ethic of passionate self-realization creates questions about the practices through which the working self is produced. If the self at work is not distinct from the self outside work, and if the value of the passionate subject lies in their subjectivity rather than in any particular competence or skill, what are the actual practices that can convert this passion into a mode of being that will be of value to employers? The answer to this question lies outside the realm of work. For passionate subjects, cultivating a working self means nurturing passionate affects in the self with the aim of maintaining intrinsic energies and passionate commitments across the whole of life. Education and training – while of course necessary for securing professional employment – fade into the background in narratives describing the cultivation of the passionate subject. Instead, there is no practice or particular area of life activity that is excluded or necessarily included in the cultivation of the passionate self. Any aspect of life can be converted into value as long as it produces passion in the self that can be mobilized and recognized at work. Instead of education, training or anything else in particular, what emerges as significant in the narratives of passionate subjects is the expression of passion and the occasional need to reconnect with one's passion after experiencing a setback.

There are two main ways in which the passionate subject creates passion and mobilizes this energy at work. The first is through personal relationships, which if managed properly will facilitate authentic self-realization at work and can be mobilized for the cultivation of value.

The cultivation of passion through personal relationships is critical to all passionate subjects, but was particularly significant for Maxine for whom the capacity to manage relationships was critical to her day-to-day work and to the creative energy she brought to her labour:

> 'I mean, a lot of times what I do doesn't feel like work because it just feels like I'm just being who I am at the moment ... I mean, you can't always choose who you work with and stuff but yeah. I have created a world for myself that I surround myself with people that I want to be around.'

Ideally, the passionate worker can be who they are at work, and the management of personal relationships at work is required to maintain the continuity between work and life that is the basis for the ethic of passionate self-realization and for the successful conversion of passion into a valued working self. In the following narrative, Adrian responded to a question about where he found motivation:

> 'So the passion that I carry throughout my social scene, which has a strong sporting involvement, and through to my career, is my underlying passion would be activating opportunities for others ... I have maintained that in a sporting sense by adopting positions of leadership because I was then able to activate opportunities for OK, let's get a sponsorship grant to buy X equipment. In a social scene activating opportunities – I would often organize a holiday for friends for example and just activate an opportunity to socialize, get out, cut loose – whatever. Then I bring that into the social – sorry, into my professional scene as well by my current role of being client relationship management opportunity – activating opportunities for them to either increase sales or improve customer service. It is that passion for constantly helping others achieve their potential that gives me future drive.'

The cultivation of passion through social relationships inside and outside work aligns with claims made in theories of immaterial labour about post-Fordist value being created from life itself, or the economization of the affects that constitute routine sociality for post-Fordist subjects. In this narrative, Adrian's value as a passionate worker comes from his position in his social life, effectively converting his relationships outside work into a source of value and into himself as a subject of value to the labour force. He positions himself as a passionate subject throughout the whole of his life, but foregrounds his social life in particular as a source of passion that he then brings into the 'professional scene' of his work. His desire here is to 'activate opportunities' for himself, his friends and also his clients. This statement aligns with the ethical commitment to creating value for others that is intrinsic to the passionate self as described earlier, while also describing the way that passions outside work are mobilized in the cultivation of the working self. The need to be passionate was also described as driving the way that passionate subjects managed their social relationships outside work, and facilitating passion for others is also seen as supporting the success of the passionate worker:

> 'If they [others] don't know what they're passionate about, I sort of make it my quest to help them through that understanding process, even to the point of at times I've lost mine – I didn't really know what I was – and by helping them discover theirs has made me think about what I want, about what I'm good at, about how I can use that to my strength...
>
> 'I feel that that particular skill set then transcends not just my career but also my extracurricular and my home life and my sporting life, because I really like to be surrounded by people. I think that's probably the passion that I'm working on at the moment. How can I refine my thought leadership? Yeah and be identifiable for that.
>
> 'For people to be advocates of their own energy would be awesome ... If people could value what their career is – if people could value what their family life is like – then that's going to be fantastic. How do I do that? Well, that's what I'm trying to work out.'

Here, Adrian's ethical commitment to 'making a difference' is made synonymous with passion, and underpins the active mobilization of personal relationships in the cultivation of the self as a worker. Encouraging others to be passionate spreads value throughout social life, and thereby activates passion within the subject themselves. This is one way in which the cultivation of the passionate self enrols the social life of the subject into the formation of the self as a worker. This narrative also demonstrates something important about passion that recalls my earlier discussion of passion as fate – that is, that passionate selves may at times be unaware of what their 'true' passion may be, and that this may impact on their capacity to mobilize passion at work and hence (hopefully) to achieve success in their careers. This was the case for Adrian, who went on to describe a situation in which he had been rejected for a promotion at work, a failure that he attributed to being misguided about what his true passion:

> 'At that point I thought my passion was communicating data in an informative manner, which was going back to what I was doing at my accountancy firm which is where I'd look at the information, write it up nicely, put in a pretty graph and tell a person what they could do with it or what it meant to them. So that's what I thought my passion was at that point in time. I wasn't successful at those roles – those applications as a result of other internal applicants that had applied. It forced me to again rethink...
>
> 'I was like what am I doing in all of these other roles that gives me energy? It came back to that opportunity piece – activating those opportunities ... I was like maybe that's where it is. That's when I started to research roles that were relationship management focused.
>
> 'They're starting to look for dynamic individuals that can adapt to a number of situations ... they're looking for a whole programme. They're looking for a well-rounded professional who has life skills, they have professional skills and they have energy to adapt in that role.'

This narrative expands both on the nature of passion and on the cultivation of the passionate self. Here, passion emerges as a force that is unique to the subject and yet as something that can be lost – becoming both a personal affect and a force in the world that must be engaged with. If passion is lost, the passionate worker must find their passion again, and will know that they are back in touch with their passion when they experience success and the feeling of self-realization at work. In order to find this passion and mobilize it at work, the passionate worker looks not at their career, but at the rest of their life in order to find inspiration. This participant knows that he is back in touch with his true passion when he makes another career move within his organization – a sideways move that nevertheless means that he has reconnected with his passion. There is a sense here of being destined for success, so long as the force of passion is followed appropriately and as long as the passionate subject works to facilitate passion in others.

Aside from these narratives of losing and finding passion, passionate subjects generally described themselves as simply being passionate people, and therefore not necessarily having to cultivate passion beyond living a passionate life in a general sense. However, as well as drawing on the passion of their broader social life, passionate workers also talked about practices that were more internally focused, aimed at producing passion from a more authentic relationship to the self. For example, Meg described her involvement in yoga as critical to the maintenance of her passion, and her narrative shows how the ethic of passion operates to make the cultivation of the self into a way of contributing value at work. As well as doing yoga herself, Meg had also started training to become a yoga teacher, and described the benefits of this training as offering a 'high-performance mindset', which would allow her to perform better at work:

> 'High-performance mindset is I guess just about being your best self, producing your best work. And what yoga does is help you become mindful and present basically ... helps you lower your brain frequency ... I think that's really improved my confidence levels and my communication, you know, it's harder than it looks to be doing the yoga pose as an example and then explaining what to do and all that. And the mindset benefits as well. So everything I'm doing is contributing to me being a better advisor and performing better at work.'

In this way, yoga becomes a way to become a better worker by enhancing her capacity for communication and mindful embodiment. Meg's leisure time is thereby enrolled into her identity as a worker, and deliberately connected with her level of performance and value to her employer. Significantly, Meg had also started to become aware and critical of dynamics within her workplace that had placed her at a disadvantage in her career. These included the male-dominated nature of her profession, which excluded her from the organizational networks that distributed opportunities for interesting work and work that could lead to promotion. She responded to this by intensifying her focus on herself, her levels of motivation and her mindset, aiming to manage these institutional structures through her capacity to create positive feelings in others:

> '[I want to be] someone who has a positive effect on every area of my life ... One is like my energy levels ... I know where my energy peaks are so I know when I need to meet with certain people and do certain things so I guess controlling or managing when and where people see me and what energy level I do certain things at is one part. And I think also just trying to see the positive side of things. There's nothing more draining than someone that is just constantly negative. So I want to look at the brighter side I guess and just be more positive.'

In this narrative, the affective and ethical dimensions of passionate self-realization become a way in which passionate workers negotiate inequalities and disadvantage at work. As well as a source of energy that guides the passionate worker through the labour market, cultivating the passionate self and distributing passionate affects to others is also a way of enhancing one's value in such a way as to rise above these restrictions. Alongside these internally focused practices, Meg also focused on networking and community involvement, sitting on the board of community organizations and charities in order to enhance what she called her 'brand':

> 'I'm really well known in the community I think as the young community person and I've been working this year to try to create professional credibility in how I'm seen in the community, if that makes sense?
>
> 'Like from the people that see me from my community where – I feel like a lot of them don't even know that I'm an accountant. So just to improve my brand and I guess, for lack of a better word, as a credible professional as well as someone that wants to help the community … I just, in conversations talking about what I'm doing at work a little bit more and if someone's talking about something they need that I could do at work, to bring it up … I didn't want it to be, "this relationship is just for me to get some work".'

Sarah Banet-Weiser (2012) situates the branding of identity as critical to shifts in the relationship between identity and cultural value in post-Fordist capitalism. For Banet-Weiser, contemporary subjectivities are increasingly intertwined with the logic of branding strategies, in which value is attributed through feelings of uniqueness and authenticity, communicated as part of a critical posture towards cynical exploitation as opposed to authentic self-realization. These ethical dispositions – such as a commitment to authenticity and helping others as opposed to cynical manipulation for the purpose of monetary gain – also shape the way in which Meg approaches cultivating a personal 'brand' that will add value to herself as a worker in the context of her professional career. For this young woman, improving her brand means cultivating value in ways that are experienced as authentic, spontaneous and motivated by a desire to help others. In this way, positioning herself as a credible professional takes place through a mixture of self-valorization and ethically driven self-expression. Passionate subjects are thereby distanced from the grubby materiality of self-interest while attributing moral and economic value to the self.

Conclusion

Out of all of the young people described in this book, it is middle-class subjects of passion who come closest to embodying the ideal post-Fordist worker, and who most enthusiastically commit to the relationship between work and the self prescribed by the post-Fordist work ethic. Indeed, one of the key arguments of this book is that the ethic of passionate self-realization is a means by which class distinction is achieved within the terms of the post-Fordist work ethic. While subjects of passion are the most totally invested in work, they also maintain the largest distance from necessity in their narratives about the purpose of work and themselves as workers. They achieve self-valorization through elevating themselves above the material necessity of work. Rather than working for a living, subjects of passion understand themselves as enthusiastically following a pathway towards self-actualization that is open to them as long as they remain passionate. Their being in this sense is not dependent on their doing (Bourdieu, 1984), but rather on their constant rediscovery of what they understand as their essential essence as passionate people. In this way, their challenge is to continually stay connected to passion, which is experienced as a unique and semi-autonomous affective force that flows across the boundaries in their life, infusing and contributing value to everything around them. The value of the passionate subject also overflows the individuals themselves, and contributing value to the world is seen as an ethical responsibility that also valorizes the self. In this way, subjects of passion enlarge the value of themselves beyond their own individual working lives in their practices of self-cultivation, while at the same time remaining committed to the uniqueness of their own biographical projects.

Subjects of passion are the most privileged participants in this book. They have all the resources required to support a smooth entry into the labour market, and thereby a continuous relationship between work and the self. Subjects of passion also reveal a connection between middle-class dispositions towards distance from necessity and *noblesse oblige*, and the post-Fordist work ethic itself, which promises a particular relationship between work and the self that is consistent with long-standing middle-class dispositions. However, in post-Fordism this takes a particular inflection owing to the renewed role that economic productivity plays in the attribution of personal and symbolic value. Dissolving the boundaries between work and the self is part of appearing as a seemingly autonomous self-realizing subject – a key aspiration for subjects of passion. However, this is not so straightforward for other young people who lack the capacity and historically embedded dispositions required to elevate the self above material necessity – whose being is not separable from their doing, and who have much at stake materially in the cultivation of themselves as workers. In order to understand this, the next chapter explores another manifestation of the post-Fordist work ethic, in which aspirational and upwardly mobile working-class young people cultivate themselves as subjects of achievement in order to avoid precarity and the risk of material deprivation.

4

Subjects of Achievement:
Social Mobility, Competence
and Aspiration

Transformations in the history of the work ethic are intertwined with the demands made upon workers by changing employment and labour regimes in different periods of capitalism. However, approaching the work ethic in terms of epochal shifts in the nature of capitalism can sometimes obscure as much as it reveals about the meanings ascribed to work in the formation of contemporary identities. The work ethic is not merely a dominant ideology of work to which all subscribe in the same way. Indeed, to make this argument would be to apply a functionalist logic to the work ethic and to the formation of classed identities through work, thereby ignoring the tensions and historical contradictions that shape how differently positioned young people respond to the incitement to self-realization through work. With this in mind, this chapter complicates the epochal periodizations of the work ethic to be found in the work of Weeks (2011) by exploring relationships to work, which I will suggest demonstrate both continuities and ruptures with the meanings ascribed to work in earlier periods of capitalism. While Chapter 3 described relatively privileged young people, whom I suggested constituted the ideal subjects of the post-Fordist work ethic, exploring the experiences of young people from working-class backgrounds reveals the work ethic as a heterogeneous discursive terrain shaped by the classed histories of work in different periods of capitalism. This chapter focuses on these experiences to explore what I will suggest is a new working-class manifestation of the post-Fordist work ethic, in which the promise of social mobility and material advancement made to the Fordist working class is experienced through the ontological reward offered by work in the post-Fordist present. This class-specific relationship with work produced in the context of both the classed history of the work ethic and within the material conditions that shape the post-Fordist present for contemporary youth, including experiences of unemployment and employment precarity.

In general, this chapter explores what I will call subjects of achievement. The chapter argues that working-class young people's relationship to the post-Fordist work ethic is one in which self-realization through work is manifested in concrete material advancement and social mobility that – at least ideally – takes place through the identification and cultivation of personal competences and their realization through successful engagement with work. It is in this sense a profoundly different relationship with work than the one that was described by subjects of passion – one in which the realization of the self is much more closely intertwined with material necessity and aspirations for achievement that is manifested in material success. In Bourdieusian terms, the distance from necessity is much narrower in these accounts, but the stakes in many ways are also higher for the young people in this chapter. The ethic of passion eschews material reward by cultivating the whole of life as a source for a worker's value, and the distance from necessity cultivated in middle-class young people's narratives about the working self is based on the assumption that a young person is destined to achieve some measure of professional success. In contrast, the ethic of achievement requires young people to succeed as a result of being good at what they do. Many young people expressed profound anxieties about failing to realize themselves as competent workers, or frustrations in not having their competences or qualifications recognized in the labour market in the form of good work. In this, the narratives in this chapter demonstrate how the post-Fordist work ethic is intertwined with the complex discursive terrain shaping youth and class in contemporary capitalism, including the pressure on young people to produce aspirational and forward-looking subjectivities in order to navigate structural precarity, and the devalorization of 'unsuccessful' lives in neoliberal capitalism. The ethic of achievement is therefore a highly idealized approach to work, in which classed identities are formed through an investment in the promises of the post-Fordist work ethic, despite increasingly precarious labour market conditions.

The ethic of achievement

This section introduces the key dynamics of the ethic of achievement. Like the ethic of passion discussed in the previous chapter, the ethic of achievement is a means by which young people pursue projects of self-realization through the cultivation of the self as a value-producing subject.

However, the ethic of achievement offers a different pathway towards self-realization to young people, one that is closer to the material necessities and rewards of work, but which is also ultimately more precarious and at risk of failure. For subjects of achievement, the necessity of self-realization through work is formed in the context of the contemporary emphasis on aspiration and social mobility as personal imperatives and powerful political discourses (Abrahams, 2017). As the expansive literature on class and social mobility has demonstrated, these ideas have transformed contemporary identities, creating new moral imperatives and forms of class distinction (Loveday, 2015; Burke, 2016; Burke et al, 2019). These ideas shape the way that working-class young people understand their place in the world and the legitimate futures that are meaningful to them in a competitive and precarious labour market. With these structural conditions in mind, working-class young people's articulation of the post-Fordist work ethic produced a relationship with work in which the value of the self is realized in social mobility and the achievement of concrete goals, or ambitions that avoid material deprivation and set the working self apart from others through some measure of material success. Unlike older participants in Loveday (2015), who retained a sense of working-class identity in explicitly classed terms, subjects of achievement aimed to become socially mobile through cultivating the self as a subject of value to the labour force. The following is an extended, lightly edited excerpt from Laura, a young woman interviewed in her final year of a technical certificate in event management. Laura described herself as an ambitious person, whose ambition revealed many of the central elements of the ethic of achievement:

'I'm a bit shy, but I'm very ambitious.'
'What does it mean to be ambitious?'
'I feel like I just always set goals for myself and am always striving for more. I like things that are accomplishable as well and I don't know, I just don't know really how to explain it, but I just think I am ambitious, because I can see where I need to go further and if I'm not doing that, I can acknowledge it and then set goals to go further.

'I don't know. I'm an over-thinker as well, and I have that thought in the back of my head that I don't want to be nothing. I don't want to be miserable, get up and do whatever I have to do just to pay the rent. I want to actually enjoy my life and not have to take a holiday for my life, because it's just so boring and dull. I want to work and enjoy it and not just settle.

'Yeah, like I just always look at other people and compare myself and I want to be able to say that I have that and I've done this. Just feel like I've accomplished something and not just been one of those people that have left school, done whatever, because they could get that and then that's done ... Yeah I know adults, family friends even, like a family that just have what they have and I'm too old now, I just have to deal with it. The money thing as well, I can't afford to just give up on that and try to actually get a career.

'I don't want to be one of those people that you look at them, like their parents gave them everything ... Because I prefer to have my own things that I got ... I feel a bit of resent towards people that actually do have everything handed to them, because I do a little bit to some extent, but not everything. And a lot of people have their jobs handed to them and that puts them forward before me.'

This narrative contains a mixture of aspiration, tension, anxiety and resentment that together reflect the profound significance of what is at stake in the ethic of achievement. For this young woman, positioning herself as aspirational and working to achieve 'things that are accomplishable' is a way of avoiding being 'nothing' – a statement that positions ambition at work as a condition for meaningful subjectivity in the most basic sense. She describes peers who she feels have left school and 'done whatever', or 'just settled' for what they could easily achieve, and who have then missed out on the opportunity to 'strive for more', and have the kind of career that this young woman aspires to. In contrast, Laura emphasizes her need to set achievable goals, and setting and achieving these goals is a way of distancing herself from these others who have settled for less. Aspiring to achievements at work is also a way of avoiding a 'miserable' life, in which work is idealized as a realm of enjoyment and personal investment. This is a narrative of accumulating value and some measure of distinction to the self, but this participant also confesses to a certain resentment at those whom she sees as more privileged than herself, who have success handed to them or who achieve prominence more easily than she, who was looking for work at the time of the interview and feeling insecure about her future despite her profound investment in her career. This resentment demonstrates the precariousness that these young people feel despite their adherence to the post-Fordist work ethic, and the high stakes of a relationship to work in which success is opposed to being nothing at all.

The need to 'strive for more' is also reflected in this comment from Tim, an 18-year-old young man in his final months of schooling who was discussing his ambitions for work in the future. Tim emphasized that he wanted more than 'just a job'. Here, he situates success at work in terms of the cultivation of uniqueness, which allows him to stand out from others:

'I just couldn't – I just feel like I'd have to – I don't know. I think it's kind of like everyone's got a thing; you look at a basketball player – their thing is to be really good at basketball. Yours is being academic with this. Everyone's got a niche, and I just think I just need to find a niche.'
  'How are you going to know if you've found a niche?'
  'You start kicking arse at it, probably.'
  'If you ended up just working a job, rather than having your niche, what would that be like?'
  'Depressing. You'd be like – you'd feel like you're not unique in your own way, I think. The niche is what makes you unique, I think. It sets you out from everyone else. You work in a Pizza Hut when you're like 50 – I couldn't do that ... I like the idea that everyone can stand out in their own way.'

One striking element of this narrative is the way that Tim aligns the cultivation of personal uniqueness with success at work, and with working jobs that are more prestigious than relatively widely available forms of work such as fast food. In this, work is described as a realm of autonomous self-realization that at least holds the potential for personal distinction – for being set apart from a mass of others. Taken together, these two narratives intertwine the cultivation of the self with personal uniqueness and social mobility, and emphasize the significance of material reward in the formation of the self as a worker. All of these are distinct from the ethic of passion in Chapter 3.

The narrative quoted at length at the beginning of this section indicates another key element of the ethic of achievement as opposed to the ethic of passion – that is, an emphasis on concrete and achievable goals as milestones signifying success. While subjects of achievement view work as a realm of self-realization and a condition for meaningful subjectivity, this takes place not through the purely self-referential process that was described by subjects of passion, but rather is materialized in the achievement of concrete goals that, as emphasized in the quote above, are within reach but constantly under revision. Aspiring to work that offered a structure for advancement was critical to the project of self-realization that subjects of achievement were pursuing in their engagement with work, and these young people described timelines and deadlines for their achievement of particular goals. It was important for these young people to be working towards these deadlines and to have their identities as workers validated in material terms. The following quote comes from Rob, a young man who had worked as a scaffolder after finishing school but had recently found work as an estate agent. He compared his two jobs in terms of the sense of purpose that his new job offered, and the kind of goals he was setting for himself in realizing his ambitions:

> 'Yeah, absolutely. You'd go to work because it was just going to work. You turn up here because you know you've got a purpose and you know you're going to go somewhere if you just keep doing what you're doing.
>
> I've set a goal. I've set a goal at the minute. I've got a goal that I want to be a listing agent in 12 months. Which will take me doing a lot of study, just knowing the right things to say and what the company's marketing plans are...'

This was also emphasized by Sarah, a young woman who was looking for work when I interviewed her, as well as studying a certificate in community services at a local technical college. This narrative is also worth quoting at length because it illustrates the role of planning for concrete goals that is so critical to the ethic of achievement, as well as situating this ethic within the material circumstances that these young people now face in the labour market:

> 'I think I kind of – I always want to be able to say, "I have just finished another qualification," or, "I have just got a promotion," or something like that. I always want to be proud of myself for what I've done. I sort of think there is no point getting to 25 and saying, "All right, I have done studying, now I'm going to work this job forever." That's for some people, but it's not for me. I'm hopefully going to live like another 60 years, so I don't want to do the same thing for the next 60 years.
>
> 'I think that more than ever the world is changing, and if I get a job today that job is probably not going to exist in 20 years' time. It will be a totally different world, so I think you have got to keep up with that and always like be open to trying something new and doing something new.
>
> '[At] 21 I was going to have met my boyfriend and we would be married at 23 and having kids at 25 and by then I would already own my own house and have a big flash car and I was going to have a million dogs. Then, once I have had the kids, I'd keep working on my career and hopefully be like a manager, or high up in the levels.'

For Sarah, the need to achieve concrete signposts of success or personal development is related to a desire to feel proud of her achievements in the world. A desire for pride in one's accomplishments is not foregrounded as a part of the ethic of passion described in Chapter 3, but is critical to young people for whom a sense of personal value is at stake or under threat in the formation of the self as a worker, and whose working identities are formed in the context of structural precarity. Indeed, in this narrative the ethic of achievement – or the sense of always striving for markers of material success – provides a means by which young people can attain a sense of narrative coherence amid what this young woman emphasizes is an uncertain and rapidly changing labour market. Like the ethic of passion, this makes the project of self-realization into a way of navigating the world of work. However, the ethic of achievement is distinctive in always referring to ambitions for material success that go beyond the cultivation of the self as such. Moreover, the first participant quoted in this section as well as many other young people discussed here also mentioned the financial rewards that they hope will flow from her ambition to realize a distinctive and materially successful career. The ethic of achievement positions financial comfort and material success as key goals in engagement with work, and it was common for subjects of achievement to discuss ambition and aspiration in terms of financial rewards. The following participant, Leah, was working in sales at a building company, and she spoke highly of her workplace as a place that facilitated her ambition to take 'the next step' in the organization and to buy the nice things that her wages now allowed:

> '[my next step] is to be a consultant ... the youngest consultant ever there has been 21 ... And she works for us, and she's pretty awesome. She's always like "No, you need to do it before you're 21. Before 21." Everyone wants everyone to succeed. Everyone wants everyone to be the next step ... When I came to [this job] I was to be consultant before I was 21, so the youngest they've ever hired anyone is 21 years old. They are like "Oh, wait until you're 21, but it'll probably be next year." They don't think that because I'm young I can't do it ... Everyone's scared of me. Everyone's like "You're going to eat us all for breakfast" when I'm a proper consultant, and I was like "Yeah, I will be."
>
> 'I think I'll be in this forever ... I think the money is just too good to not want to be ... Some people are like "Money's not everything" but I'm like "I like nice stuff."'

Again, in sharp contrast to subjects of passion, subjects of achievement were clear about their desire for financial reward as a signifier of success at work, and many discussed the importance of being increasingly well remunerated as part of their ambitions for the future. Subjects of passion can skirt delicately around the issue of remuneration to position themselves as interested primarily in personal development and in helping others because they are making comfortable salaries or are reasonably confident that they are destined for well-remunerated work. In contrast, subjects of achievement see money as an issue that is at stake in their future – a reward for the successful cultivation of themselves as subjects of value to the labour force and a signifier of success at work.

One way of accumulating value to the self that goes beyond material reward but was specific to subjects of achievement was the cultivation of a reputation – or social recognition from others as a hard worker who produced good work. A reputation as a good worker was seen to come from a personal dedication to work and a commitment to being 'the best' within a given occupation. This was articulated by the following young man, a builder's apprentice:

> 'I want to be the person that tries to go a bit above and beyond, to have that reputation. You're still thinking or doing stuff relating to work in your home life. Not consuming your whole spare time, but contributes to your work to make you a better worker ... you're just more dedicated to it, especially – even just planning that afternoon and what you're doing the next day. You're just thinking about it, the way you're going to do it ... you want to be the person that's recommended. It's pretty hard to be the best. You want to be up there. You want to have a good reputation that people can confidently say this bloke's work is good.'

One of the key things about a concern for reputation as part of the ethic of achievement is that it positions the value of the self at work in terms of being a 'good worker' – someone capable of producing a superior product. This draws attention to the final key element of the ethic of achievement, which is that the rewards of work – understood here as experiences of self-realization intertwined with social mobility and material reward – are seen to reflect the competence of a worker, or in other words the fact that a worker is 'good at' their job. This is distinct from the ethic of passion, which goes beyond particular competence or the possession of particular skills to position the whole of life as a source of value. In contrast, in the ethic of achievement, what matters is that a worker works hard and is good at what they do – cultivating skills over time that are specific to the task and that qualify them to succeed and receive the rewards of work. In the words of Bourdieu, the subject of achievement's 'being' is produced through their 'doing', rather than to anything essential to them. Elise was studying at a technical college at the time of the interview and described an unpaid internship she was currently doing in terms of the 'ego boost', or the sense of accomplishment that came from successfully completing work tasks:

> 'I've got no experience but she trusts me and says, "I need you to do this, this, and this." And it's up to me to do it and make it perfect. And I feel a sense of accomplishment and it boosts my ego a bit, which helps in, I don't know, being successful? Yeah.'

All these elements are brought together in the following narrative from Trish, a young woman interviewed for the second time after she had recently finished a diploma of event management at a technical college and found a job at a local bank working in customer service and sales. Her narrative intertwines a concern with reputation, a love of work, ambition for materially recognizable success and a sense that her competence will underpin success now and in the future:

> 'To do good in this job role you know I feel like even just making like a reputation for myself, like letting people know that I do good at what I do and you know I try hard, yeah.
>
> 'It feels like how everyone says do what you love, etcetera, etcetera. You actually want to come here and at the moment I'm wanting to learn and I can't wait to already know everything about it and just already thinking about moving up and stuff, it just makes you want to do better and better. That's definitely like a career and you see yourself doing it, not just for now. You see yourself doing it for ages. I feel like it will be forever, but you never know. I feel like I can only just keep going up here ... as far as I know it goes, supervisor, branch manager and then it goes up to your head office and then it's your regional managers and your CEOs and then other sections and stuff like that. The tier is huge of how many people.
>
> 'I feel like I'm good at it ... it feels good. It makes you feel good when you've done something correct or you're completely good at it.'
>
> 'Given what you're doing now do you feel successful?'

'Yeah. I do feel successful.'

'What makes you feel successful?'

'Probably the fact that I've got a position that I actually wanted in corporate. Corporate events is where I wanted to go to. I never wanted to do weddings or festivals or anything like that. So getting into a position like this, a full-time job and having a full-time job itself is also exciting for me, to achieve something like that and also the company. To work for [this bank] itself, I'm pretty pleased with that. So I find that quite successful and to finish my diploma as well, not everyone does it.

In this narrative, the sense of competence – of having done 'something correct' – is brought to the fore as part of the broader relationship between a personal investment in the self and the material milestones that signify the successful realization of the ethic of achievement. This narrative also recalls the broader precarity of the youth labour market in its relationship with education, in which completing a qualification and moving into a relatively secure full-time job is itself regarded as a significant success. In this context, Trish feels that she is cultivating a reputation within her organization as a competent worker who can for this reason anticipate material success in the future. Authentically representing the competence of the self – understood in terms of discrete skills and task or job-specific capacities – was the key means by which subjects of achievement approached the job market, including applying for work. While subjects of passion tried to represent themselves as broadly passionate in all areas of life, subjects of achievement were focused on representing their skills or, as Clara who had recently been to a job interview at a local bank put it, what they can or cannot do:

'What you see is what you get with me. I don't see the point in pretending to be something you're not, especially when it comes to jobs. I'm not going to sit there and say I can do this, I can do that, and then I get into the job and I can't do any of it and they're sitting there going crap, what do we do now? There's no point. I was very honest with them, in the sense that I told them things that I couldn't do and things that I could do.'

With all these elements, the Fordist promise of material success and social mobility through labour is intermingled with the emphasis on self-realization through work that is so critical to the post-Fordist present. This reflects the history of the work ethic in different eras of capitalism and different regimes of accumulation. Indeed, some subjects of achievement aligned their own aspirations with those of their parents, but intertwined a traditional emphasis on the moral value of work in itself with the aspiration for work that offers enjoyment and status on the basis of personal competence. Josie was one example of this:

> 'Yeah, well, I know I definitely don't want to end up like my mum. I feel bad saying it, but she hates her job. She only goes there because like money. She feels like if she doesn't, everyone else is like, oh, you stay at home, you're a bludger [lazy person]. I love my dad's attitude towards work. He always put 110 per cent in. He's like, even if you don't love it, you're there, so you have to make that commitment. That's very much me. If I'm there, I will make the commitment ... He was like, if I'm there, I want to be the best ... That's very me. If I'm doing something, I'm doing it 110. I'm doing good at it.'

By opposing the worker who always goes above and beyond to the figure of the 'bludger', the commitment to work that defines the 'respectable' industrial working class is given a post-Fordist inflection, becoming the basis for an approach to work that mixes dedication to work with aspiration.

The key elements of the ethic of achievement include competence, material success and social mobility, as well as a certain uniqueness in relation to a broader mass of others who have 'settled' for low wage or menial work. The promise of the post-Fordist work ethic articulated through the ethic of achievement is that aspiration, hard work and competence will result in financial rewards and increased social status. In this way, these young people avoid what the first participant quoted in this chapter described as 'being nothing', in which a failure to actualize the self as successful in work means a failure to achieve meaningful subjectivity at all. In its emphasis on social mobility and material success, the ethic of achievement resembles the Fordist work ethic as articulated by Weeks (2011), in which the industrial working class was promised material comfort in exchange for adherence to industrial discipline. The emphasis on social mobility also takes on a post-Fordist inflection in its emphasis on personal achievement and on self-realization as a reward for work, intertwining the material rewards of work with the ontological rewards of the post-Fordist work ethic. The result is a deep personal investment in achievement through work, in which aspiration and ambition underpin the possibility of satisfaction in life now and in the future.

In what remains of this chapter, I discuss the practices through which subjects of achievement aim to cultivate themselves as workers, and the tensions that arise from young people's adherence to the ethic of achievement. This is discussed in relation to how subjects of achievement understand the value of the self to the labour force, how the work ethic is used to make sense of setbacks in education, training and labour market engagement, and how the aspiration to social mobility impacts on existing relationships with family and friends.

Cultivating competence amid precarity

The practices that young people use to cultivate working selves are part of the way that the different manifestations of the post-Fordist work ethic define the relationship between the self and the capacity for economic productivity. Chapter 3 showed that the ethic of passion located the capacity for value across the whole of the passionate worker's life, which meant that nominally unproductive practices as diverse as yoga and team sports were understood to contribute to the value of the passionate worker. In contrast, subjects of achievement understand their value to the labour force in terms of their competence – their capacity to perform a particular realm of work-specific tasks better than others. What matters for subjects of achievement is that they are 'good at' what they do. In essence, this means that the cultivation of the working self takes place through a kind of reflexive process in which young people work to find something about themselves – a particular attribute or personal characteristic – that they can cultivate into a competence that will be recognized as such on the labour market. Moreover, for subjects of achievement, education is critical to the cultivation of the working self. This certainly reflects the long-standing assumption that educational success will lead to social mobility, as well as the explosion in post-compulsory educational attainment among young people from all social backgrounds with deindustrialization and the emergence of the immaterial economy. It also reflects what Jessica Gerrard (2014, p 871) has described as the 'learning ethic', in which the moral obligation to cultivate labour power via the work ethic is enacted through education, and in which notions of 'lifelong learning' come to stand for the constant self-improvement required of contemporary workers. However, what is critical for the purposes of this book is the way that educational credentials fade into the background in the ethic of passion, whereas for young people in this chapter the ethic of achievement shapes young people's approach to education in critical ways.

Writing about working-class relationships to education and social mobility, authors such as Burke (2016) and Abrahams (2017) have shown that working-class students tend to focus on the value of an educational qualification as providing skills that will be valued on the labour market. Abrahams (2017) argues that this forms part of a discourse of 'honourable' mobility, in which a good job is a meritocratic reward for hard work, qualifications and skills. However, understood in the context of the post-Fordist work ethic, this emphasis on the cultivation of skills takes place within a specific relationship between work and the self in which young people aim to cultivate competence. The following excerpt is from the first interview I conducted with Trish, whose second interview I quoted earlier, which took place in her final year of her qualification in event management at a technical college. Prior to studying for this diploma, Trish had tried to go to university, but had found the teaching styles alienating and had struggled to support herself financially, in part owing to a lengthy commute from home to university. In this narrative, she begins by describing her experience of studying, and then discusses the attributes of herself that she feels have facilitated the successful completion of her diploma:

> 'Well, yeah, I mean you've got to be able to take charge and everything like that, I just always was the organizer like, for ages as long as I can remember, even with my family, I would take that off my mum because I would want to organize this and I kind of have a passion for it and am quite good at it, like being on time, getting everything ready and then I was like, I can actually do something with this ... I like being in control ... Telling people what to do, I mean I can handle being told what to do but I would prefer to be the, like I, that's why I would be in management, I'm the type of person that has to have things a certain way and yeah, definitely in authority.
>
> 'I think there's like this will probably be like one of the first things in my life maybe just excelled at so well, like I've just, every single assignment, every single like presentation, even like volunteer work I've just gone bang, bang, bang and it just comes naturally and like, even like you know you feel like there's like signs when you're on the right track, like everything seems to be flowing well and good, like when at uni it just seemed like too hard and life was just making it so hard to do it and get there and but here I was like, cool, I'm doing like actually good, I'm on the right track so yeah.'

Here, Trish reaches reflexively back into her biography to find experiences that relate to personal attributes she feels are helping her succeed in her studies. She describes herself as someone who enjoys being in control – organizing family occasions and telling others what to do. In this narrative, this attribute is a rationale for her decision to leave university and study at technical college, where she has experienced more success. In her words, these studies have 'come naturally', and from her perspective, her success in her studies reflects the way that she has mobilized her personal attributes towards an industry and qualification that can capitalize on these personal strengths. Another participant recruited from the same technical college course in event management credited her interest in the course to the fact that she too was a 'controlling'-type person, a designation made as a result of a personality assessment task that she had undergone in her final year of schooling as a result of careers advice:

> 'I think it was in Year 11. Just basically asked you – it was like rate this out of five how likely you would be to enjoy this task ... A little bit about your personality as well and stuff like that. I don't know what it's called but I'm pretty sure it was like a – I think it was from the board of studies ... Yeah so obviously if you're not an outgoing person you wouldn't be in a teaching job or something where you have to talk in front of people.'
>
> 'So is there a particular part of your personality you think that made sense for you to go into this course?'
>
> 'Yeah, controlling ... I like organization and stuff like that and I just had an interest in the planning as well as the actual events ... Yeah like I don't like it to be – things to be like messy and not organized at all.'

It was not uncommon for participants to discuss psychological tests or exercises while at school as helping them to discover something about themselves that they felt might be useful on the labour market, and using the results of these exercises to choose post-compulsory courses. In general, however, these narratives about education also foreground the necessity of competence for success. In fact, it is in the cultivation of competence into skills that are recognized as such on the labour market that the mode of self-realization intrinsic to the ethic of achievement is best expressed – as the realization of attributes into valued skills, typically through post-compulsory education. Moreover, aside from formal education, the practices described by subjects of achievement as contributing to the cultivation of themselves as workers were focused primarily on volunteer activities that directly and obviously contributed to their work:

> 'I done registration which is like registering people into an event which is like event work, I worked at [a music festival] … you know like registering the artists in, so I was back in artists' area, I registered them in and made sure that they were like ready to go on stage, anything they wanted was kind of like they'd ask me, I'd get it. Yeah, it was such a great experience … I've done like volunteer work here and then heaps of conferences…'

Unlike subjects of passion, for whom almost anything could be enrolled into the formation of the working self, subjects of achievement who cited activities beyond formal education always did so in ways that were directly linked to work itself. These activities were also not described in terms of personal development or a broader concern with a personal 'brand' (cf Burke et al, 2019), but rather concerned the accumulation of skills and experience to list on a CV. Clara spent time volunteering at a local police station as a person assisting juveniles who had been detained by police, and described this volunteer work as contributing to her particular skills in the following way:

> 'Customer service, clientele – anything really working one on one with clients. It's pretty much what I do at the police station when you break it down … We just monitor them in the police station and make sure they're being looked after and if they're not, we do something about it … It's experience, yes … It's tailoring programmes to suit each client's needs, and that's where I thrive … Anything is experience, and the more experience you've got across the board, the better.'

Aside from building up educational qualifications and experience, Tom also felt able to pinpoint a personal attribute as underpinning his enthusiasm for the job, even one as general as being 'good at talking':

> 'Oh, mate, I was with the scaffolding, not really by choice I suppose … I was just working with dad just to get some extra coin and that. I was trying to figure out what I wanted to do and then he actually mentioned to me one day, he said, I reckon you'd be really good at real estate because you're good at talking to people. You can talk to – you just talk heaps and

I was just like yeah, yeah. No worries I'll go give it a go … I
went around all the agencies here and just like, I'm looking for
work and Noel took me in and I went to a bit of an interview
process and got me to the end of the tunnel and it was yeah,
it's good, I'm loving it now.'

So while the ethic of passion views all a worker's life as a source for value,
the ethic of achievement maintains a distinction between the productive
and unproductive dimensions of the self, and requires young people to
identify particular personal attributes in order to realize a productive self.
In a sense, this requires more reflexive work from young people in order
to connect some aspect of themselves to the labour market. Rather than
operating on the assumption that everything can be converted into value,
subjects of achievement must decide on something that they are likely
to be good at, and then mould this personal attribute into a skill that
will be valuable at work. However, it also means that their subjectivities
are less subsumed by the disciplinary requirements of post-Fordist work.
The aim is not to subsume one's entire subjectivity into work, but to find
some useful part of the self that can be made to create value in the labour
force and to cultivate this attribute into a form of competence. This is
a reflexive process that takes place in relation to actually existing labour
market opportunities and educational institutions. These are attributed
with meaning in terms of the relationship between competence and
material success that makes up the ethic of achievement.

However, this process does not always work in the way that young
people hope, and the experiences of autonomous self-realization offered
by the post-Fordist work ethic are not necessarily so easily accessible.
Despite their enormous investment in education and in work, and despite
their aspirations to experience the unique modes of self-actualization
offered by the contemporary work ethic, subjects of achievement often had
to reassess their future. Most commonly, this was because of experiences
of unemployment or a pragmatic reassessment of the employment
opportunities available to them. However, for some it was as a result of
a feeling of mismatch between themselves and their aspirations. Felicity
described her excitement at getting into university to study midwifery
and her disappointment that she did not feel a connection to her studies
or her work placements, which had resulted in her leaving the degree:

'Because I was upset that I didn't like midwifery. I really
wished I liked it but … It's just a respected job, it's a close little
community job, you see people being born. Like, it's amazing,
incredible, and I mean you get to learn. Like you just get so

much knowledge through uni about the body and all these cool science facts and, I'm missing out on all of that. Yeah, because I didn't like it. I guess that's why I really do wish that I liked it … I was absolutely over the moon when I got my offer. I was calling everyone, I was so stoked. It was one of the happiest moments, ever. Because it's a selective course … So I was so excited that I got in. And about four weeks into it, at that four-week marker, I was just like…'

In response, Felicity went to study marketing at technical college, and was taking further qualifications in order to create her 'own' university degree, one that would be more flexible and allow more labour market opportunities than her midwifery qualification:

'Yeah. So I've done marketing, which would be very handy. And I'm thinking about doing project management at TAFE, as well. But in 2018 they offer an interior design and a decorations course, so I'm thinking about doing that, as well. So, I'm kind of making up my own university degree to get to where I want to be, whereas, before I had no idea. I was only 18 and I didn't want to think about work, really. Now, I'm like, "All right."

'I feel like as long as I've got these certificates of marketing, and then interior design, project management, I could go into so many things. I could be a marketing manager and that could be for cinemas and all sorts of things. So I just feel like, as long as I've got experience in the same kind of business field and creative field, but lots of different pathways I can take.'

This narrative demonstrates the feeling of contingency that ordinary young people had to cope with when the coherent narrative offered by the work ethic was disturbed, in which education or work failed to offer the forms of self-realization promised as a reward for a personal investment in work. Again, the ethic of achievement here is more precarious than the ethic of passion described in Chapter 3, precisely because of the additional contingency and precarity that these young people face. The chances that things will not work out are high, as are the stakes if young people abandon the work ethic. One important aspect of this process, and another way in which subjects of achievement differ from subjects of passion, is that the reflexive cultivation of the working self is always narrated with an eye to the availability of jobs. Tim described himself as the person among his group of friends whose aspirations had once been most clear, but was in the process of reassessing his aspiration to become a journalist after becoming pessimistic about his job prospects:

> 'I was so dead set on that journalism thing, and then to find out oh they're cutting all these jobs and then probably how it's such a cut-throat kind of thing. That kind of pulled – made me go recently – because that was in the last – probably start of the year I've kind of gone – because out of all my friends I was the kind of the one that knew what I wanted to do, and right now I'm just kind of like, aargh – don't know ... I don't really want to pay all that. Since the government's raised all the university fees, you don't really want to go on – that's probably the one thing me and Mum agreed on most; you don't want to go on a degree and pay all that money and then have nothing to come out of it, really ... Yeah, you've got a flashy thing on the wall saying you can do this, but you're not actually doing it.'

Like many working-class students, this young man was averse to debt, especially if his job prospects were uncertain. His aspiration to go to university had thereby been placed into doubt, creating anxiety about what his future would otherwise hold. Laura (quoted earlier) had moved to pursue a university degree in science, a decision that she attributed to her capacity for problem-solving and her interest in the natural world. However, she abandoned this degree after deciding that she was unlikely to find work in science in her local area – an assessment that was almost certainly correct, but was made without considering the possibility of moving (see Farrugia, 2019 for a broader discussion of the relationship between place and work for young people in this project):

> 'Yeah, I moved to [a nearby city] to do a science degree. I'd always been interested in science and then I did year 10 work experience in a milk factory, of all things, in the lab there and I loved that work. I went to [the city] to do that, but about halfway through the first semester I realized I'm probably not going to get a job in [my local area] and it was probably a silly idea, which Mum had been telling me for months before I went, but I did it anyway.'

Despite abandoning her university studies, Laura maintained her adherence to the ethic of achievement. She enrolled in a range of certificates, including one in community services that she was studying when I first interviewed her, and continued to set goals for herself that would signpost her success. However, she was also unemployed and living with her parents, which was creating conflict and a sense of dependence. As she progressed in her studies, she became increasingly anxious that she was not meeting the goals she had set for herself:

> 'It's important to me to keep studying and always, I guess, making myself better. When I have finished the Cert IV, I want to get like an entry-level job just so I am working, making money and can start the career and then keep studying.
> 'The other day I had a bit of a meltdown because I realized I was running out of time to do everything in the schedule that I set out for myself when I was young, but I think that's just part of it and I will be able to do what I want to, but it's probably going to take a while and it won't be as easy as I thought it was always going to be.'

While setting concrete and achievable goals is critical to the ethic of achievement, for Laura these goals became a source of anxiety rather than a way of measuring the realization of the competent self. These experiences – of anxiety, frustration and the curtailing of aspirations – reveal the highly idealized nature of the work ethic, especially the expansive promises of the work ethic's post–Fordist manifestation. In mandating self-realization through work, the post–Fordist work ethic sets high expectations: achievement, constant upward mobility and internally driven success. A failure to live up to these expectations creates a sense of looming disaster. In the words of the participant whose narrative opened this chapter, the possibility of failing to self-actualize through work means just settling for whatever is available and abandoning the rewards offered by the successful realization of the work ethic. This is a possibility that constantly threatens the aspirations of subjects of achievement. However, the work ethic also offers a response to the possibility of failure, which is to redouble one's efforts in the cultivation of the working self. The quoted participant's narrative of 'making myself better' through educational credentials and an ongoing adherence to the ethic of achievement is an example of this process, responding to feelings of failure by continuing to enhance one's value for the labour market.

To explain the ongoing adherence to the work ethic despite the struggle to find work, it is important to keep in mind the way that the work ethic operates as a moral imperative, intertwining personal worth and the capacity for economic productivity into projects of self-realization that are ethically mandated in the formation of young people's identities.

Adherence to the work ethic, and embracing the rewards that the work ethic offers, is critical for moral subject formation in the most general sense. This is explained by Felicity, also quoted earlier, who was in the final stages of her certificate in event management at technical college and had been looking for work with little success. In this narrative, her personal investment in work that goes beyond merely wanting 'a job' is counterposed to those who are less invested in work but who are successful regardless, creating feelings of resentment towards others who are not grateful for their success and will not use their jobs as opportunities to personally develop:

> 'Yeah, I want it to make me happy and feel fulfilled and not just a job. I don't want a job.
>
> 'My career I kind of have to start with hospitality kind of things and there's people that are just doing those hospitality jobs to have a job. So it's harder to get in there. There's people that just want it, because they want money, whereas I want it because I need it to actually get to the goal. Which is frustrating, because that last interview I went to, a girl in my class actually got the job and she said after that I don't actually like events any more, so I was like that's really annoying, because I would have used that job and it would have actually helped so much … I wouldn't just be like oh this is just like a random hospitality job, because I want money or because I need a job. It's because I'd actually want it to progress more and not just be like this is the bare minimum that I'm going to do.'

For Felicity, aspiring to personal development through work is a guarantee of being a 'good worker', as opposed to those who merely want 'a job' and who would therefore be likely to put in the 'bare minimum' at work. In this sense, ongoing adherence to the work ethic on the part of young people who experience setbacks such as unemployment or who are otherwise forced to revise their aspirations is a way of continuing to position themselves as subjects of value to the labour force. Making the personal commitment to work that is mandated of good workers allows young people to see themselves as having prospects and as deserving success. This mixture of moral obligation and honourable aspiration is key to the way that the ethic of achievement operates in the formation of working subjects, even in conditions that may challenge the optimistic narrative of self-realization articulated by young people who have successfully followed its prescriptions. While Chapter 5 will explore instances in which the work ethic broke down in young people's narratives about themselves and employment, those who remained subjects of achievement in the face of challenging conditions reflect the uniquely powerful role of the work ethic in shaping relations of moral worth in contemporary capitalism.

However, cultivating the self as a subject of achievement can create tensions for young people, in which the aspiration to social mobility leads to social distance between themselves and their friends or family. While middle-class subjects of passion talk about networking as a way of attributing value to themselves and those around them, subjects of achievement are in a sense more individualized, owing to the emphasis on meritocratic aspiration, personal hard work and competence (see also Abrahams, 2017). Rather than cultivating the whole of their life towards work, subjects of achievement sometimes felt that they had to distance themselves from those around them in order to achieve the kind of distinction that the work ethic offered. This was articulated by Sarah, who also positioned herself as aspirational in contrast to friends of hers that she felt had settled:

> 'A lot of my friends work at takeaway shops and like, I'm not degrading that, or anything, but I don't want to do it, it's not for me. They've always been like, "There is a job going, do you want it?" I'm like, "Well, sort of, because there is nothing else, but I want to try and find something better, just retail, or something." It's really hard to say to them, "No, I don't want that job," without offending them … I get it's for them and it suits them and they're happy, but it's not for me.
>
> 'Yeah, a lot of them all started working the same time I did, in year 9, sort of like year 10, 11 they all had dreams. One friend, who works at Hungry Jacks, she was going be like a criminal detective, something like that, they all had dreams they wanted to do, but they sort of just never have got around to it. Yeah, they're happy just working where they are.'

Throughout the interview, Sarah often prefaced her comments by saying that she did not wish to appear 'stuck up', but that she was also not willing to work in the kind of jobs that many of her friends worked in, and had experienced some tension with her peer group as a result of her aspiration for 'something better'. For Josie, these tensions were connected both to class and to gender, in which the work ethic gave her a means by which to resist pressure from her family to follow traditional gendered pathways. While still at school, her parents encouraged her to become a primary school teacher, which they said would allow her to balance work and motherhood more easily, and offered a more secure pathway into a job. However, Josie aspired to work in hotel management, because she saw it as a high-status job in which people would not necessarily expect to find a young woman with a dominant personality:

> 'I just feel I like the fact that I'm more direct and in charge. It's more of a dominant place where there's not as many – like there's females, but it was never like a female can be in charge kind of thing. I like the fact that it's like something where people aren't expecting it. When they see a female in charge, some people are, ooh, like what? I like the fact that I can prove to people like they're wrong ... I feel like I'm very different to most of my friends, because they're not very like – I'm very like bossy. If I want something, I'll get it where all my friends are like, oh, just go with the flow, like whatever happens happens. I'm like, if I want to get that grade, I will get that grade.
>
> 'They're very just like – they don't like big dreams. They're very like a small family. We don't talk to our neighbours and really keep to ourselves, but I don't want to be like that. I'm the opposite. I feel like I'm pushing them to expand. I'll do things and they'll be like, oh, that's not what we're used to. Or I'll be like, can I go here? They're like, oh, we don't really go there.'

For this young woman, the ethic of achievement is a way of positioning herself as aspirational in opposition to the gendered and classed expectations of her family, while still maintaining an adherence to the moral significance of work and to personal development through work that is mandated in post-Fordism. Despite her commitment to work as such, Josie reported substantial conflict with her family over her aspirations, in which their desire for a secure pathway within a commitment to motherhood conflicted with her desire to assert herself in what she saw as a relatively prestigious occupation that transgressed local gendered expectations. In this as in the other narratives of tension quoted, realizing the self as a subject of achievement produces tension and conflict with intimate others, in which the cultivation of value in the self transgresses established expectations of suitable pathways for 'people like us'.

Conclusion

The ethic of achievement is a class-specific manifestation of the post-Fordist work ethic that demonstrates continuities and ruptures between

Fordist and post-Fordist working identities. Many aspects of the Fordist work ethic as described by Kathi Weeks (2011) can be found in the ethic of achievement. The emphasis on social mobility as a reward for work is one critical example, which combined with the emphasis on competence creates a narrative in which material advancement and increased social status are the reward for working hard and well. However, these features are given a new inflection through post-Fordist emphasis on the cultivation of the self and on work as a realm of self-realization. Through the ethic of achievement, young people must find an aspect of themselves that can be cultivated into a skill, or a realm of competence that can be identified and then turned into the capacity to create value at work. Self-realization within the ethic of achievement thereby consists in cultivating a competent self and having this competence reflected in one's material advancement, conceived as a never-ending process of personal development. This shapes young people's practices of labour market engagement and – critically – their relationship with education as well, in which educational credentials (acquired with an eye to the labour market) are seen as facilitating the conversion from a personal competence to a skill, and thereby to the capacity to be good at what one does. Within this relationship to education, the ethic of achievement is pursued through concrete goal-setting and reflexive biographical planning designed to realize the self as a subject of value despite precarious social conditions.

The ethic of achievement also encompasses contemporary pressures connected to employability, notions of 'aspiration' and the meritocratic ideology that underpins the political celebration of social mobility. These pressures are intertwined within the dynamics of post-Fordist work. Adhering to the ethic of achievement means responding actively to the contemporary pressure on young people to raise their aspirations in order to reap the rewards offered by the contemporary world of work, and to work on themselves in order to maximize their value to the labour force. Understanding these discursive processes in relation to the ethic of achievement demonstrates how they are taken up by young people in specifically classed ways. In particular, the narratives in this chapter suggest that notions of aspiration and employability have become intertwined with the long-standing promise of social mobility as a reward for work that has historically been key to the Fordist work ethic. While notions of employability and aspiration are (rightly) critiqued for their role in reproducing individualistic understandings of the relationship between young people and the labour market, in the ethic of achievement they become part of a broader emphasis on social mobility that has long been part of the way that working-class people are encouraged to relate to work. Their uptake by young people in this chapter shows one of the ways in which these discourses contribute to the formation of youth subjectivities – that is, by contributing to the ethics through which young people are formed as workers and thereby as classed subjects in their relationship with work.

5

Socially Appropriate and Credentialled: The Struggle for the Working Self

The post-Fordist offer of happiness and self-actualization through productivity rests on fragile ground. The narratives of self-realization through work discussed in this book so far idealize work as a realm that welcomes young people's authentic selves, and that will confer value upon youth subjectivities as long as workers make the personal commitment to work that the work ethic requires. This promise is perhaps impossible to realize even in the best of circumstances, and longitudinal evidence suggests that work declines as a priority for young adults with more labour market experience and with the onset of other life commitments, such as intimate relationships and family formation (Andres and Wyn, 2010). In this sense, a total commitment to work as the key priority in life may be specific to young people with less experience in work, for whom the cultivation of employability is a live and pressing concern. However, the narratives in preceding chapters also reflect an intensification of young people's personal investment in work and productivity precisely as precarity and unemployment have become normalized in the youth labour market. This is particularly the case in the research sites explored in this book, which are economically peripheral locations in which youth unemployment is a topic of frequent public discussion. While the work ethic makes cultivating the self into a means for navigating labour market uncertainty, the promise of meaning and value through an earnest commitment to work becomes more obviously mythical as young people experience protracted periods of unemployment, or when the material realities of working practices in demanding, demeaning and poorly paid occupations make the myth of work as a realm of autonomous self-realization impossible to sustain. Drawing on these experiences, this chapter explores what happens when the post-Fordist work ethic meets the insecurity and degradation of actually existing working situations in the youth labour market.

In general, the chapter describes the struggle to form a relationship with work when it is experienced as a hostile social environment in which the value of the self is unrecognized or made impossible to actualize. Degradation, low-self-worth and anxiety are all long-standing aspects of experiencing unemployment in the work society, and have been documented throughout the Fordist and post-Fordist periods (Sennett and Cobb, 1972; Nolan and Whelan, 1996; Lamont, 2000). This chapter situates these consequences in terms of the work ethic, exploring what happens to young people's ethical relationship with work when authenticity and self-realization through work is made impossible, and when work becomes a realm of devalorization rather than authentic self-expression. The narratives that follow come from young people who experienced protracted periods of unemployment, despite attempting to cultivate a productive self in line with the precepts of the work ethic, or who worked in situations that were unfulfilling or degrading – terms that describe much of the employment available in the low-wage service economy. Their social backgrounds varied, some beginning in families similar to those of the 'ordinary kids' in Chapter 4, and some coming from backgrounds of profound economic precarity. Some of these participants had begun with aspirations similar to those described in Chapter 4, hoping to succeed at work by mobilizing a personal competence into a recognizable skill. Others had experienced both education and work as a hostile and alienating environment from a young age, making the concept of authenticity at work remote to their experiences and position in the labour market.

In this chapter, I approach young people's responses to this situation in terms of tensions at the heart of the work ethic in its relationship with the contemporary youth labour market. Young people described a variety of practices designed to position themselves as employable and morally valued workers. One strategy included studied efforts to cultivate the appearance of being an appropriate and properly disciplined worker, and the accumulation of credentials that would facilitate a flexible response to the emergence of opportunities for employment, should these arise. Rather than aiming for authentic self-realization, in this third relationship to the work ethic young people aimed to be socially appropriate – 'good workers' who would be reliable, presentable and hard-working. Accumulating credentials was not a way of cultivating qualities into skills, but rather a way of preparing for a variety of working situations in the hope that something would come up in the indeterminate future. These credentials were sometimes mandated by welfare interventions designed to maximize the employability of unemployed youth. For many, the outcome was feelings of degradation and personal inferiority, as work consistently failed to live up to the promises of the work ethic. The chapter concludes by discussing the failed promise of the work ethic and exploring the significance of experiences of unemployment and workplace degradation for theorizing the relationship between work, productivity and the self in contemporary capitalism.

Credentialled and socially appropriate

When I first interviewed Andrew he was 21 years old and living with his partner and her sister in Mildura. Both he and his partner were unemployed. Andrew's mother was a casual cleaner at a local hostel and his father worked at a factory not far from the city. Andrew had been unemployed since he finished school, which he left when he was 17 after twice failing to pass year 11. While Andrew experienced compulsory education as alienating, he nevertheless began by approaching his entry into work in a similar way to young people described in Chapter 4 as subjects of achievement – that is, by enrolling in a technical certificate in an area that he felt would nurture a pre-existing competence. In this case, Andrew described a long-standing interest in electronics and a talent for fixing electronic goods that he had developed since his interest in them as a child:

'I'd love to work with electronics or even installing stereos and stuff in cars.

'I [can do] hardware repairs. So something ... fails or stuffs up I'll work out how or why ... I haven't really done PCs for a long time but DVD players, CD players. I do laptops occasionally ... I've been doing it since I was, say, ten years ... My parents actually wouldn't pay to get the Play Station fixed because my brother kept breaking it. So I turned around, because they bought me a second Play Station and they still kept the old one that he stuffed up first. So I'm like, OK, I'll pull the old one apart first, put the two together to make one good one and ever since I've been working with them ... I've actually done electrical things as well, which is in the caravan I used to live in. Like, I rewired most of it.'

The certificate that Andrew enrolled in was vocationally oriented and reflected his interests and skills. In this sense, Andrew had done everything right in the cultivation of himself as a worker, identifying a personal interest or competence and then entering post-compulsory education in order to enhance his employability. However, his family was unable to financially support him while he studied and he was unable to find the work he needed to fund the course, so he was forced to drop out with a few months of study remaining in order to search for work. Eventually, Andrew was forced to enrol with a welfare provider charged with supporting him in finding work and monitoring his conduct as a 'job-seeker' in order for him to remain eligible for unemployment benefits:

> 'I completed Year 10 but failed Year 11 twice. So I left school and was doing my Cert III in Electronics but I couldn't afford to keep paying for it. So I started that course but I haven't actually finished it and after that it was looking for work. I completed a Cert II or III in Job Skills, whatever with [an employment service provider].
>
> 'I just finished training in the Cert II in General Education for Adults ... Something to fill in time, looking for work still.
>
> '[Right now] I'd really prefer anywhere because I want to get somewhere because sitting at home doing practically nothing is boring ... I'd like to work as much as I want, as much as I can ... It gives me something to do rather than walking around the house in circles most of the time.'

This narrative is typical of the experiences of young people in this chapter, many of whom left school with aspirations for satisfying work that slowly dissolved when they were unable to find employment. Unable to complete his training in electronics, Andrew soon abandoned his desire for work in this area and began applying for everything he could think of, including jobs in fast food and in retail outlets, such as supermarkets. After an extended period of unemployment, Andrew enrolled in a series of certificates in general education at the local technical college, in part because his unemployment benefits were made conditional on his engagement in these courses and in part as a way of alleviating the boredom of unemployment. These certificates included basic literacy and computer usage skills, which were not helpful in assisting him to find employment and held an uncertain value.

Like Andrew, Paul had been unemployed for over a year when interviewed, and had abandoned his aspirations for work that matched his interests, shifting from something he 'can develop' to any low-wage service job he could find as he struggled with mounting debt:

'I started off at more banking and admin, but now I've put in for the works, back at [supermarkets]. I've put in for McDonald's and anything I can get. But I haven't heard anything back from any of them yet ... anything goes at this point ... I was in that mindset of I want something I can develop. Then, as the weeks and months went on and I'm desperate, I'll take anything at the moment and develop on something later.'

As these two participants demonstrate, the material exigencies of unemployment mean that the desire for self-realization becomes a remote concern. Instead, young people described becoming increasingly despondent and anxious during their experiences of unemployment, as the aspirations that the post-Fordist work ethic mandates dissolve in the face of the unavailability of work. Participants described constantly applying for jobs and receiving no response, unsure of why they were unsuccessful. These experiences were discouraging, and left young people without any clear way forward in their engagement with the labour market. Aside from applying for work, participants also described their involvement in a range of short courses and certificates offered by welfare organizations or technical colleges that did not seem to have a clear relationship with either the young person's biography or identity, or with the job opportunities available to them – as this narrative from William describes:

'So I was really keen for the [service of alcohol certificate] and [service of gambling certificate] ... But I [also signed up for] a certificate in businessing ... I'm glad I did, because it's actually come in really good, and I'm enjoying that ... So yeah, [my social worker] lined me up with it, and it's an extra paper. And then yeah, I was doing a Cert III in Business as well as my RSA [responsible service of alcohol] and RSG [responsible service of gaming] ... I'm gathering, you know... [Carl].'

Will had gained the certifications required to legally work in pubs and venues with electronic gambling machines, as well as a certificate in business administration suggested by a social worker provided by an unemployment service provider. He describes 'gathering' certificates while unemployed, and enjoyed these courses because they differed to his experiences of school, which he experienced as infantilizing. However, these certificates were accumulated without a clear plan in mind as to why they would be useful or how they would relate to the self, although he and other young people hoped that they would increase their chances of finding some kind of employment (a hope that was also encouraged by social workers and unemployment service providers). Rather than accumulating these certificates in order to cultivate competence into achievement (see Chapter 4), these young people took advantage of any opportunity to acquire a credential, hoping that these would increase their chances of landing one of the many jobs they applied for every month.

This investment in credentials is exemplified vividly by Lisa, whose parents were contract cleaners, and who when I first interviewed her was enrolled in:

> 'Three main courses and four short ones ... So Certificate III in Hospitality ... A Diploma in Community Service at [technical college] and then Child Care Cert III online with Open Colleges, [short courses in] OH&S, advanced leadership, training essentials and auditing.'
>
> 'Why are you doing so many things all at once?'
>
> 'I am not settled down and it's the opportunity. I did do the childcare last year and just carrying over. I did Cert IV in Community Services last year so I just thought do a diploma because I don't have much experience and they said I won't be able to find a job because of my age and not much experience, go and do a diploma, you've got more of a chance getting a job.'
>
> 'You don't struggle to juggle it all?'
>
> 'Yes, I've had my moments. It usually shows when I crack at night. I get – Argh!'

As this narrative suggests, Lisa had qualifications in childcare and community services, but had gone back to study in a range of areas after being unable to find a job, and was accumulating credentials in hospitality and doing short courses in skills such as auditing. She was unsure of where any of these certificates would take her, but felt compelled to fill all her spare time with study. By remaining productive in this way, Lisa described efforts to build her self-confidence after feeling marginalized at school:

> '[on her auditing course] I just wanted just the knowledge. I thought I've got a little bit of time on the Saturday, let's go ... you have to do the other units later on to get the full qual. But at the moment I'm thinking some extra units won't hurt me.'
>
> 'Is this a strategy to eventually get you work or is this just out of interest or...'
>
> 'Both and at the same time give me self-confidence, like I stick to stuff and I know I can do it despite the hard times ...

Well any time a certificate comes I'm over the moon. It's like yes I really worked for this.'

Lisa's investment in education recalls elements of the ethic of achievement, including the sense of tangible accomplishment that comes from having gained a qualification. Her narrative also draws on the 'learning ethic' (Gerrard, 2014, and also discussed previously in Chapter 4), reflecting the moral imperative to constantly improve the self through education in order to prepare for the labour market. However, her narrative and approach to work is uncertain and fragmented, aimed as much at increasing her self-confidence as cultivating skills. Her experiences of education and work were characterized by anxiety, and Lisa was frantically involved in a range of activities that she hoped would build her confidence and change the way in which she related to others. In this sense, she was focused less on becoming skilled and more on becoming socially appropriate – someone who could present the image of an appropriate worker. This included leadership training courses provided by a local community organization that focused on her embodiment and relational capacities, which she considered a critical job skill:

'For a quiet person it's a bit nerve wracking ... I was always quiet at school ... kind of just left behind ... I stuck it out though.

'It's kind of like all the underdogs – I surprise people sometimes. One of the teachers thought I just go home and I do nothing, stay at home. She said to my mum "why don't you let your daughter go out ... and just be with friends?" Then she said "but she does swimming and dancing, girls' brigade, play the piano. When does she have time to do all this?" Then she's like "oh wow". She was shocked at how busy I am.

'When I did my [leadership training] ... [I] do a lot of public speaking, how to move with purpose, how to ... Use your hands – hands can be distracting as well and your eye gaze as well. I'm really bad at it. Also doing some job skills like being able to not stand too close to a person but far enough away ... I had some good praise so I was happy ... With the eye gaze we had to stand in front of the group and not smile for a whole minute, just look around and people just nod back. A lot of people broke into laughter. I just stood there and didn't fidget.'

In one sense, Lisa's discussion here recalls aspects of Skeggs's (1997) discussion of embodiment and respectability for working-class women, in which value comes to be read and experienced through aesthetics and the body in a specifically gendered mode of classed embodiment. In post-Fordism, embodiment and relationality come to the fore in new ways, becoming part of definitions of value connected with employability. For Lisa, the enormous number of certificates, short courses and other activities she was involved in were aimed at shaping her bodily comportment and interactive style, which she felt were deficient in ways that were preventing her from finding employment. Vanessa had recently found work as a supermarket cleaner through a labour hire company, and also describes her efforts to obtain this job in terms of a deliberate bodily comportment designed to convey social appropriateness:

> 'You've got to dress very nicely and speak appropriately…so I made sure all my tattoos and everything were covered up and I dressed quite nicely. [My partner's] sister mentioned to me that they like hearing the word 'efficient' and stuff like that, so I tried to use it as much as possible. I had a resume ready to give to them like she suggested as well and a handshake before I left.'

In this sense, Lisa and Vanessa experience work not as a realm for authentic self-expression, but as an unfamiliar social environment that they must engage with in a studied and careful manner in order to present the right impression. Rather than authentic self-expression, here Vanessa's emphasis is on good manners, and on conforming to a set of interactive rules that she hopes will result in an 'appropriate' self-presentation that will be accepted by potential employers. Vanessa's focus is not on being authentic but on 'getting it right' by deploying relational styles and modes of personal presentation that she feels are alien to her but are necessary to the positioning of herself as a presentable worker. Her experiences are also profoundly aestheticized, focused on being confident and nicely dressed – a delicate balancing act aimed at cultivating herself as an appropriately feminized working subject. Work for these young women is a profoundly alien environment in which their identities are not attributed with value. Instead, work is an exterior realm in which they must perform themselves according to rules that remain opaque to them but reflect the long-standing devalorization of working-class femininity. These young women must 'get it right' in order to find work, and they anxiously reflect on what this means as they search for jobs. Julia articulates this well when discussing what she feels employers are looking for in a worker, in the context of preparing for an interview for a job in a bar:

'I feel like it's personality, but at the same time they want you to answer the questions right. It's hard to prepare, especially when you don't know what they want from you, because especially this one tomorrow the job description wasn't that detailed. So obviously I know what wait staff and bar staff is, but the actual expectation of what kind of people they want. And especially since it seems like a fancy kind of place ... it's a bit hard for me personally to display my actual personality.'

There is a sense here of not knowing the 'rules of the game' (Bourdieu, 1990), and Julia's unfamiliarity with the modes of interaction deemed 'right' by employers is narrated alongside a general anxiety about her ability to display her 'actual personality' – a display that she is unsure will be received well regardless. For Rebecca and Chloe (twin sisters interviewed together who were searching for work at the time of the interview), a hesitance in displaying the self in job interviews was intertwined with a long-standing working-class suspicion of those who were too enthusiastic about displaying their own value to others:

Rebecca:	'I had one at [a large supermarket chain] and there was about 20 something people in there. You don't want to speak out and talk yourself up in front of other people, it's really uncomfortable ... I prefer group [interviews] but then I don't speak up because I'm like someone else will talk or answer that question.'
	'Do people speak up?'
Rebecca:	'The weird ones ... This chick in Big W like actually Googled things about Big W like she had a notebook...'
Chloe:	'I think she actually got the job, though ... just like when they ask you questions and you've got to speak up and I'm like well I don't want to be cocky and talk about myself in front of like 20 other people I've never met before ... I'm like I don't want to be cocky and then they go well she's up herself when it's only like 30 minutes. I have to be up myself and I'm really not.'

These participants exemplify the increasingly disjunctive relationship between the subjectivities required of the post-Fordist labour force and a habitus that does not lend itself to self-expressive performances of one's own personal value (Skeggs, 2004). However, rather than taking this for granted or, in Bourdieusian terms, making a virtue from their exclusion, participants such as Lisa and Vanessa described a need to alter themselves in various ways in order to successfully become workers – to cultivate new forms of affectivity and relationality in order to become employed. Indeed, when asked about her hopes for the future, Lisa focused on her affective and relational capacities, for instance hoping that she would be better at taking phone calls in a professional manner, and thereby demonstrating to herself and others that she could become employed:

> 'At the same time I want to prove them wrong and myself ...
> I'm preparing myself for the workforce and getting all the skills [but] I'm not fully equipped ... answering the phones I find tricky. But I'll get there.'

However, when I interviewed Lisa again about a year later, she had finished all her qualifications and certificates but was still unemployed. She had searched consistently for work in childcare and in the hospitality industry, but had been unsuccessful. At this time, her feelings of exclusion from work had intensified, and while she was considering further qualifications, she lacked a clear sense of where these new qualifications might take her or how they related to her own identity:

> 'I don't know if I'm ready to work just yet. Because I don't know if I want to get back into study ... I was looking at laboratory skills, for a laboratory technician.'
> 'OK.'
> 'So it's like, one of those, "How does it fit into everything?" "Just because."'

In this context, she described feeling like an 'outsider' and having to develop resilience in order to persevere:

> 'That's me ... I'm not a clear-cut person ... I'm not in the same boat as everyone else. That's what I feel like. I feel like an outsider.
> 'I don't fit the norm. I work myself hard, and people notice, but don't always say ... Mum goes, "You'll find out what it is later on. Just stick with it, get through it, that's what jobs are like." I just have to keep going. This is developing a character, now... Like, resilience. If it goes badly, keep going back.'

Lisa's feeling of being an outsider captures the fundamental dynamics at play in the formation of the working self for young people who have experienced substantial periods of unemployment or disadvantage, and sums up the narratives from young people in this chapter so far. In narratives such as those from Andrew, the practices and subjectivities formed through young people's engagement with work shift from the ethic of achievement to a pragmatic acceptance of the necessity of work of any kind, as well as the frantic accumulation of educational credentials with a dubious relationship to the labour market and no narrative connection to young people's identities. Young people such as Lisa and Vanessa who have experienced substantial unemployment do not narrate themselves in terms of value to the labour force, and do not have ready narratives about the role of work in the actualization of the self. Instead, work is a realm in which their identities are unwelcome and unvalued. Trying to find employment means cultivating not authenticity but social appropriateness – the image of the good worker. At the same time, young people must work to maintain a sense of self-confidence, a trait that is prized among contemporary workers and yet difficult to maintain amid constant rejection in the labour market. The aim here is to produce a credentialled and socially appropriate self who can present the appearance of value without seeking self-actualization through work or realizing the value of the self in employment. Here work becomes a realm of risk, representing a threat to the self that is made necessary by the material exigencies of unemployment.

Governmental interventions and crafting the employable self

As reflected in some of the narratives so far, Australia is similar to other post-Fordist economies in its increasingly expansive and punitive regulation of unemployment and the conduct of the unemployed. Sociology, specifically the sociology of youth, has examined the government of unemployment extensively as an aspect of roll-out neoliberalism (Peck and Tickell, 2002), in which the government of unemployment takes place through efforts to craft self-responsible and entrepreneurial individuals (Kelly, 2006) and the implementation of benefit sanctions for those who do not conform to workfare regimes (Adkins, 2017; Haikkola, 2019). Interventions have also emerged that instruct unemployed young people in the cultivation and transmission of positive affect, in which the deliberate creation of a pleasing demeanour becomes a critical aspect of employability (Friedli and Stearn, 2015). Recent Australian public debate has also come to focus on the activities of private employment service providers contracted by the state, who have been accused of failing to address the needs of clients even when these are imagined within the narrow discourses of employability and human capital characteristic of neoliberalism. Narratives such as the following were common in this project from unemployed participants:

> 'I went through [a provider] and I had one meeting with them and they were like, "Look at our website, there are some jobs and we'll contact you when we find you a good job." Then that was it. I got a message from them every Tuesday saying that I have missed an appointment that I didn't know about. I'd ring on Monday and say, "Do I have an appointment today?" They'd be like, "No." Tuesday say, "You have missed your appointment." That went on for six months, or something, and that was it, that was the whole contact with them.
>
> 'They'll check it out and that's about it. I haven't heard one back yet and I've been with them for over a year … I'm going there for literally nothing, but the thing is I'm going there. If I don't go there I don't get paid … Basically it's appointment after appointment, always fixing stuff through Centrelink and if it's not Centrelink it's [employment provider].'

Experiences such as this created a sense of hopelessness and a feeling of being constantly under siege, subject to the competing and opaque demands placed upon young people in job searches, job interviews, and mandatory activity and reporting regimes. However, young people generally entered into programmes designed to support them to find work in good faith, as well as with feelings of desperation brought about by long periods of unemployment. Something similar can be seen in MacDonald et al (2001) who have described this as a game of snakes and ladders, with young people in areas of high unemployment and precarity being shuffled through training schemes and placements with no clear benefit to themselves and no clear pathway into employment. In this project, responses to these programmes varied depending on the kind of intervention that young people were subject to, including training in bodily comportment and 'confidence', personality assessments to advise on the sort of work young people might be suited to, and routine disciplinary interventions based on ensuring young people applied for enough jobs per week to satisfy their welfare obligations and sanctioning young people for failing to attend appointments. As Zoe discussed, these interventions were rarely successful in supporting young people into jobs:

'So, you looked for work for two years.'

'Yeah, it was a long time ... I had to do a programme for a few weeks with [service provider] to stay on [unemployment benefits] ... it was just like, this lady came ... and it was just, "People get jobs with interviews" and being confident and stuff like that.

'It was helpful, but it didn't really help me get a job. It was helpful, though ... We had like booklets and we played – kind of little games and like talking in front of a group, that's what it maybe was about, talking and stuff like in front of the groups.'

'Did it help you in terms of work?'

'No, you see, I thought I was doing better in my interviews, but obviously I wasn't.'

Aside from demonstrating the ineffectiveness of employability interventions in finding work for unemployed young people, Zoe's narrative shows that the emphasis on deliberate embodied performativity as a way of cultivating employability and value in the self is also a part of the government of unemployment and the ways that unemployed youth are encouraged to relate to work (cf Friedli and Stearn, 2015). In these interventions, young people practised confident speech and bodily comportment under the guidance of employment specialists in the hope that this would increase their attractiveness to employers. Young people with experience of these welfare interventions also described various kinds of quizzes or personality tests; here they are discussed by Chris:

'We did like a personality test thing, and there was red, blue and green. Red means assertive and my way or no way. I know the green is chilled out and do what you're told. The blue was something else. I got blue and green, so, I was pretty much laid back and do what I get told to do ... They look at your résumé and look at what type of person you are and your personality and stuff, and then they pick the place that they think will best suit you.'

Chris suggested that these quizzes had made him think differently about work, abandoning his initial aspirations to seek apprenticeship as a mechanic and become more open minded about his future employment. In this case, the personality quiz had encouraged him to feel more positive about the work experience he was about to begin in a warehouse:

'It's teaching me to have an open mind and try different things. Just because you've got your mind set on one thing, doesn't mean you might not like doing another ... I'd never thought I'd work in a warehouse ... after you look at it all, it's not as bad as you think.'

These governmental interventions reinforce the relationship to the work ethic described by young people here. Interventions encourage young people to produce the kind of careful presentations of self that were discussed as important by Lisa and Vanessa, while also abandoning pre-existing aspirations for work in favour of seeing themselves as having a flexible range of suitable working futures related to their personalities. While these are assessed through personality tests of various kinds, they inevitably position young people somewhere in the low-wage service economy, usually in ways that maintain long-standing gendered assumptions about suitable work for working-class women and men (cf Simmons et al, 2014). Moreover, these interventions do not encourage the cultivation of personal qualities into skills or a relationship to the self in terms of value. Rather than work for the sake of self-valorization, young people approach work for the sake of material necessity and to fulfil the requirements of disciplinary regimes regulating unemployment benefits. In this sense, young people's engagement with unemployment services reflect their ambiguous relationship to the post-Fordist work ethic – within the work society but abject to the modes of self-valorization available to young people, as discussed in Chapters 3 and 4.

(Un)employment and the degradation of the self

The remainder of this chapter explores instances when the threat of degradation through work is made real in the lives of employed and unemployed youth. The primary focus of this section is two interviews I conducted around 18 months apart with Vanessa and her partner Rob, who lived together in an outer suburb of Newcastle. During the period of the project, Rob worked in the bakery of a large supermarket, while Vanessa had worked a number of precarious jobs, experienced substantial periods of unemployment and when I first interviewed them had just found work as a cleaner in the same supermarket her partner worked in. Their experiences highlight the profound contradictions that emerge when work is positioned as the critical realm of subject formation and for the realization of the value of the self in a context where employment is precarious and often unsatisfying. They also make the notion of self-realization through labour visible as an ideological fiction that sustains increasingly expansive forms of exploitation in the youth labour market and causes profound suffering for those who are unable to live up to the moral edicts of the work ethic.

Rather than relating to work as a project of self-actualization, Rob described falling into bakery work as a result of failing to find work as a mechanic.

> 'Well I was actually wanting to be a mechanic, but it was on the radio that bakers wanted jobs and I wasn't having any luck, so I just applied at the local one at Thornton because that's where I lived. Yeah, I got a trial there and when I was doing my week trial there another place rings me saying "oh, you can have this spray-painting job if you want it". I'm just like "oh, I'll get back to you". I talked to the boss at [this bakery chain] and said "I like this", because I was actually enjoying it. Do I definitely have it? He said "yes". I said no to the other place and then I was a baker.'

Initially, Rob described enjoying the work, in particular the tactile sensation and satisfaction of working with dough, and after an apprenticeship at a national bakery chain he found work in the bakery of a local supermarket, also part of a national conglomerate. However, this work required him to work hours that are unsociable, difficult to manage and constantly changing, and he did not feel that his pay was worth the impact of these hours on his life, health or relationship. Rob was under no illusions about the meaning of this work for him or of his value to the company, and said that he and his co-workers were often reminded that they were expendable and replaceable. Despite this, he had no other work experience and felt stuck as a baker forever:

> 'I've had the same speech from the store manager a few times. Apparently people would love, you know, to be a baker here. He has people lining up to be a baker ... Pretty much, you know, just reminded. In a sense he's saying, "Yeah, you're replaceable", without saying that.
> 'I still do apply for [other] stuff ... But I don't hear anything because all it says on the résumé is I'm a baker ... [I apply for] anything that's not baking.'
> 'So you're sick of it?'
> 'Yeah ... I have been for years ... But, you know, I've got to pay the bills somehow.

'Another thing also I like to say to people is ... you're just a number. Because you have, like, your own pin number, you have your own ID number. So pretty much we're all just numbers being told what to do by other numbers ... Everyone's replaceable, yeah. Like, my manager has her own numbers; she's a number that tells me, a number, what to do. Even the actual store manager he's just a number getting told what to do by another – by another number. That's all it really is ... Everyone's replaceable. They let you know that.'

Work here is explicitly described as profoundly alienating – a context in which workers must abandon any ownership of themselves or their subjectivities for the time that they are working, and can recover these when they leave work. This is in line with the classic account of alienation from Marx, in which 'the worker only feels himself outside his work, and in his work he feels outside himself' (Marx, 1978, p 74). Neither the promises of the Fordist or post-Fordist work ethic have any relevance here, and Rob and Vanessa are neither subjects of passion nor subjects of achievement. Indeed, Vanessa and Rob felt no desire to invest themselves in their work beyond what was necessary to maintain a reasonable level of material comfort, and there was no sense in which they would have liked work to take on a more expansive role in their life than what was encompassed by Rob's bakery work and Vanessa's casual cleaning and maintenance. Discussing the personal demands of work, at one point Rob mentioned that the supermarket chain 'takes your soul':

Rob:	'[supermarket] takes your soul ... It does. They expect a lot from you, they do.'
Vanessa:	'They expect you to devote everything to them. Every company probably does, but as soon as [they] stuff you around or they expect you to stay an extra few hours or whatever, everyone ... says "welcome to [supermarket]". And that's just what everyone says to you if you get stuffed around ... They expect everything.'
Rob:	'Yeah, every time you clock in they take your soul ... Your soul is theirs until you clock out ... But if you're not at [work] they think that you're at home next to your phone waiting for a phone call. That goes from, like, casual to full time. Just if they need to contact you they think you're going to be there and, "Hello" ... You're theirs when you're there. Like when you type

> in your thing, that's you giving them like your soul
> and when you punch out you're taking your soul back.'

This narrative reiterates the cynicism and alienation running through all Rob and Vanessa's narratives about work, and demonstrates how the degrading and precarious nature of low wage service employment impacts upon young people's lives and working identities. During the first interview, Rob felt trapped in his identity as a baker, and while Vanessa was happy to have found work after a long period of unemployment, she was under no illusions about how rewarding her work as a cleaner was likely to be. Nevertheless, she said that she had thought about trying to find work as a real estate agent, since she felt that this might be a nice job that would allow her to present herself in a manner that was both professional and allowed for a greater degree of self-expression than her work as a cleaner:

> 'I'm just looking for a job – because every job I've sort of
> done so far, I can't wear my jewellery. I can't wear certain – I
> can't wear my hair a certain way ... so I'd just like a certain
> job where I can look nice and presentable and I don't have to
> be hard labouring jobs, or like hospitality's hard work as well.
> So – and I've thought you know, I wouldn't mind going into
> real estate and just opening up a house and showing the house
> so I thought it would be a nice job.'

However, when I interviewed Rob and Vanessa a second time their circumstances had changed, and Vanessa had lost her job – effectively as a result of disciplinary interventions made by unemployment agencies. She described not receiving enough hours in her cleaning work to survive materially and supplemented this income with a small amount of support from unemployment benefits. However, she was told that she must find a second job in order to remain eligible for government support. She found work at a chemist but was treated poorly. She was then fired from her cleaning work because of her second job, and then fired from her second job without explanation soon afterwards:

> 'At the end of every shift I did [at the chemist] I got told I
> was no good ... I learned a new cash register system in a day.
> I never stuffed up. I learnt how to file scripts. Even when
> there was no one in there I was going around tidying shelves
> making it look like I was busy, but still at the end of every shift
> I was getting told I was no good. Which really did not make
> me feel really good at all. Then I told [the supermarket] that,

"Sorry, you know, I can't do Fridays any more, I'm doing it at the chemist." He said, "Well, if you can't do what I want you to do you're no longer needed."

'Then not long after that the guy at the chemist rung me up one day and said, "Look, you're just no good. We don't want you." I said, "Well, are you basically telling me I'm fired?" And he said, "Yes." I said, "Well, thank you" and hung up the phone. So I was jobless for a good year and a bit and I was getting to the point where my depression and anxiety started playing up again because every job interview I went to was getting turned down.'

As a condition of receiving unemployment benefits, Vanessa was expected to apply for over 20 jobs per fortnight, and as she remained unsuccessful she became increasingly anxious and depressed – widely acknowledged consequences of long-term unemployment (Shamir, 1986; Carson et al, 2003). As a result she was transferred onto a disability payment, but was still expected to search for work:

'I just started going to them and they're, like, "Well, you've got to do I think it's 23 jobs a fortnight; find 23 jobs a fortnight and then if you get work you need to be doing 20 hours a week or something." I'm, like, "Well, I can't actually handle that at the moment because of anxiety." Because sometimes I'm out in public and I just have a panic attack and there's no reason for it … I'm getting there, I'm just not where they want me to be at the moment. It's actually causing me more stress and I've been breaking down and crying every week before I go to [meetings with the welfare agency] and that because it's just too much.'

As time went on, Vanessa described attending multiple job interviews only to be unsuccessful, and the internalized feelings of worthlessness that came from her inability to find work:

'I was getting to the point where I said, "Can" – I told my job seekers, "Can you ring them up and ask them why I did not get the job? Please tell – tell them to tell me what I'm doing wrong so I can fix it." It was getting to the point where I just felt like it was me; I was getting rejected. It was just me. I just got to that low point where it was, like, I don't want to look for jobs any more because there's something wrong

with me ... I don't even want to look for work any more. I
just don't want to do it. I'm sick and tired of it. I tried and I
tried ... Nothing good's come out of it.

'It's at the point where we're not happy. We're just living.
We're paying bills.'

The experiences of Vanessa and Rob amount to a process of slow but
inexorable degradation, in which work becomes a realm of alienation and
devalorization, and is experienced as such in no uncertain terms. While
the work ethic encourages young people to relate to working practices
in terms of value and authentic self-realization, this kind of subjectivity is
impossible to sustain when employment is degrading and unemployment
seems impossible to escape. Nevertheless, when work is positioned as critical
to the economies of value that shape the contemporary self, it is difficult
to avoid feelings of worthlessness as a result of being excluded from work,
despite the profoundly alienating working situations that these two young
people have experienced. This tension – between alienation at work and
worthlessness in unemployment – is critical to life in the 'work society', in
which the notion of self-realization through labour makes work necessary for
self-valorization despite the deliberately devalued status of precarious labour.

Finally, when work becomes a space of degradation, aspirations come
to focus on material remuneration, respect and respectability. Chloe had
worked at a fast food chain for six years, a job that she started while at
school. She described feeling embarrassed about her work, including the
way she was treated by customers and the general working conditions
of her job. In this context, she described a desire for an 'office job',
the attractions of which mostly centred around material comfort and
general decency:

> '[Fast food chain] ... It's pretty crap ... It was my first job, so I
> went from just my casual shifts and then I was struggling to do
> both that and school so I left school at the end of year 11 and
> started working more shifts before I became full time because
> there's not many day staff available and then yeah I just haven't
> found a new job ... It's embarrassing too like I'm embarrassed
> to work there ... I'm just sick of the place completely, six
> years is enough ... see I'm not the type of person that has like
> lifelong goals. I'm more of a, I'm happy to ... get a decent
> job, work ... You know, I'm not like I want to do this and do
> this job ... Like yeah I'm just happy to work.
>
> 'I don't know, I would just like an office job. Something
> quiet, where I can sit ... I run around eight hours a day, every

day, like I want to sit down. I want an air conditioner … I just got to pay my rent … as long as yeah I'm happy and making enough money to live.'

For Chloe, an ideal job means getting out of fast food – an industry that she associates with immaturity and poor treatment – and into a respectable position with a comfortable working environment where she can make enough money to pay her bills. This is a pragmatic response to work as an environment that threatens the value of the self and in which the material necessities of life are placed at risk by poor remuneration and precarity. The necessity of respect is also at the forefront of this narrative from Todd, whose employment history consisted of spells of precarious work and unemployment in the years since he left foster care and who had a casual job cleaning and detailing cars at the time of the interview:

'A normal wage is supposed to be $20 an hour. For a young teen you would only get $10 to $13 an hour … They don't even know about it until they start asking questions. That's not really giving us a fair go or the motivation to keep working.

'You have to be paid for it. You have to get paid for the respect that you have done. You can't just sit around and do nothing. You have to really pull work to a full potential.'

While he emphasizes the moral significance of hard work in this narrative, Todd's focus is on working conditions that respect the disciplined labour of the worker. These narratives from Todd and Chloe represent the desire for basic security and a haven from the hostile working conditions they have experienced throughout their working lives thus far. Moreover, an emphasis on remuneration and respect at work also means that the separation between work and the rest of social life is clear and important in these young people's lives. If work is a realm of degradation, then it is critical to maintain a separation between the self at work and the self outside work, otherwise the devalorization experienced at work defines a young person's identity.

Vanessa: 'I prefer the perfect balance between home and work, like I'd like to enjoy my job when I go to work and get paid a nice amount and then be able to have enough time to come home during the week and do things, like clean the house and go shopping and stuff like that. But yeah, it's hard to find a job like that.'

Rob: 'I'd love to not do anything and get paid. That's not happening.'

There is no sense here that work is or should be the key signifier of the value of the self, or that work offers either achievement or passionate self-realization. Instead, accepting the unfortunate necessity of work, the ideal job is narrated as one that is well remunerated enough to maintain a materially comfortable life and is insulated from the worst excesses of contemporary capitalist exploitation. Once work is over, the remainder of life can begin again, ideally without too much interference from the demands of casual employment.

Finding work: becoming employed beyond the work ethic

I conclude this chapter by returning to the story of Andrew, the participant quoted at the beginning of this chapter whose interest in electronics gave way to the desperation for anything going. When I first interviewed Andrew, it was hard to see how he could find a way out of a difficult and enormously precarious position. He had been unemployed for two years, his employment service provider was making little effort to assist him in finding work and he had applied unsuccessfully for every job opportunity he could find advertised online. However, when I interviewed him again 18 months later things had changed. Andrew had found work through an acquaintance, working in automated tractors used to harvest horticultural products on a large property around three hours' drive from where he lived. The work was difficult and draining, and involved sitting in a tractor for 12 hours at a time with nothing to do unless the tractor broke down, as all its movements were automated in advance. There were no skills or experience required for this work beyond working the hours required and submitting to intense surveillance. Andrew's movements and bodily comportment were electronically monitored while he was in the tractor to ensure that he did not lose focus or fall asleep, as was common among these workers owing to the immensely tedious nature of the job and the long hours that it required. Through this work, Andrew was able to accumulate some savings, which was especially significant as his partner had become pregnant and he was expecting a child, but the emotional toll of the work meant that he was even more unhappy than when he had been unemployed – socially isolated and exhausted from commuting and from the gruelling tedium of the work itself.

However, after working this in role for a few months, Andrew was able to find casual employment at a local bottling factory supervising the bottling and packaging of wine. Andrew's duties in this job consisted primarily in checking automated bottling processes and applying labels to boxes. This work was some distance from his initial aspirations, precarious and more poorly remunerated than his work in the tractor. However, Andrew described it in much more positive terms than his previous job and seemed upbeat about his current work situation and his prospects for the future. His satisfaction with this work came not from any sense of self-realization, but from being occupied throughout his shift and looking forward to his fortnightly pay cheque:

> 'So you're enjoying it?'
> 'Yeah.'
> 'What do you enjoy about it?'
> 'Always doing something and you know you're going to actually get something out of it.'

Here, Andrew's enjoyment of work is connected with remuneration and with the benefits of being employed in other areas of his life. Becoming a father was of course critical to the significance of his employment, which allowed him and his partner to move into their own apartment and furnish it in a way suitable for a young child. Reflecting on the time since he had been unemployed, Andrew also described the benefits of employment on his social life, and his general feeling of freedom in the lives of himself and his partner:

> 'It's been so much better, though. Being able to buy stuff that we want as well. Not having to buy everything you need and not having any luxuries. We have a social life even with the baby. And because out at [the tractor job] no social life at all, because the time you were home you wanted to spend with family. But now ... I can actually go out with friends, go to a friend's house, have them come over. And we actually get to go out. Rather than sitting on a phone every night because that's about all we can do.'

In her book on class, work and dignity in the United States and France, Michele Lamont (2000) describes the significance of work for the self-worth of working-class men in terms of ensuring an orderly social existence that includes the capacity to care for and support others. Lamont's work resonates in significant ways with Andrew's narrative here, in which the benefits of work are fundamentally about having the money required to maintain a comfortable standard of living and socialize with friends, and the feeling of satisfaction that comes from having moved from a situation of poverty and unemployment to the feeling that something resembling a normal life is now possible. However, having made this shift, Andrew expressed ambivalent views on the nature of unemployment itself in his local area. When he had been unemployed he described being characterized as a 'dole bludger' by others – a stereotype that characterizes the unemployed as feckless and morally inferior, choosing unemployment as a way of avoiding the disciplinary requirements of work. However, having become employed, he also suggested that there were substantial numbers of those who did in fact shirk this responsibility and chose unemployment, despite the enormously difficult situation that he himself had faced as a result of being unable to find work:

> 'It's always a big thing especially around [here], because you even see on the news the top ten dole bludger areas or whatever, [we] were number three. That's for people not turning up to appointments or whatever. And yet they still get a payment.'
> 'Did you feel like before you had work that people saw you like that?'
> 'Yeah, quite a bit.'
> 'Was it people that you knew or just in general?'
> 'The people we knew and occasionally general ... Old mates [as well] ... And then you get them people that get offered jobs, but don't actually get up and do it.'

Andrew went on to describe examples of those who had avoided work when it was available, characterizing them as irresponsible and lazy. Andrew's experiences, and his narratives about employment and unemployment, reveal a tense relationship with the work ethic and the work society. His enjoyment of work has little to do with self-realization through labour and more to do with the material necessity of employment for sustaining a satisfying life in the most basic sense. In this respect, Andrew is outside the post-Fordist work ethic as theorized in this book, having experienced first hand how the promise of self-actualization is made fictional in the context of unemployment and unsatisfying work. Andrew has also experienced stigmatization as a result of unemployment, as well as poor treatment on the part of welfare providers. However, Andrew nevertheless endorses the moral significance of work as a compulsory practice, even in circumstances where it is unavailable or degrading. In becoming employed (however precariously), he has shifted from a stigmatized position to one with a modicum of value within hierarchies of moral worth that position employment as critical to the value of the self. In making this observation, my aim here is not to criticize Andrew, but rather to highlight the profound moral significance of employment in the work society, and the ongoing significance of work as a disciplinary requirement for moral subject formation even for young people who are aware that the realities of employment do not live up to the vast promises made by the post-Fordist work ethic. Like the experiences of Vanessa above, who internalized her unemployment as a reflection of her own worthlessness, Andrew's narrative also demonstrates the individualized relationship with work that the contemporary work ethic mandates, and the consequences of this for those who experience first hand the hostility of the labour market to young people.

Conclusion

This chapter has explored the subjectivities and practices of young people whose labour market experiences position them as abject figures in relation to the forms of self-valorization offered by the post-Fordist work ethic. While they may have started as subjects of achievement, the young people in this chapter confronted structural conditions that made any form of fulfilling engagement with work impossible, including protracted unemployment and working conditions that were degrading and alienating. Rather than a space for self-realization as in Chapters 3 and 4, young people in this chapter approach work as a hostile and alien environment, the rules of which are unfamiliar and opaque. Young people struggle to comport themselves in line with these rules, often unsure whether they are getting it right and with very little reward regardless of effort. In these conditions, the practices they use to cultivate identities as workers are designed to respond to uncertainty and present the image of a socially appropriate worker – an image that is explicitly regarded as alien to the authentic self but necessary owing to the demands of work.

Becoming credentialled and socially appropriate is not an ethic of self-realization in the sense described in Chapters 3 and 4, because it does not include a definition of the value of the self that is realized in practices and labour market experiences. Young people's experiences have not encouraged them to see their identities as holding value to the labour force that can be realized in working practices. Instead, the aim here is to demonstrate conformity to rules that are experienced as extrinsic to the self, and to aspire to employment that minimizes the degradation that is involved in submitting to the requirements of work. The value of work therefore lies not in the cultivation of the self, but rather in the necessity of a wage for maintaining a decent life outside work. The decency of this life is not defined in terms of social mobility as in Chapter 4, but rather in terms of the ongoing maintenance of immediate personal relationships and the ability to manage the expenses of life without a sense of immediate crisis. There is also no discussion of a desire to be 'successful' in the way described by subjects of passion or subjects of achievement, since these manifestations of the post-Fordist work ethic position the notion of success in terms of realizing the value of the self, whereas young people in this chapter see work as something that stabilizes the rest of life. Instead, young people hope to secure employment that does not threaten their self-worth (defined in non-economic terms) and is relatively materially secure.

The experiences documented in this chapter reveal a number of contradictions within the post-Fordist work ethic in its relationship with contemporary class inequalities and actually existing labour market conditions. First, from the perspective of this chapter, the post-Fordist work ethic is an ideological fiction, a myth of self-realization through labour that is made visible with attention to the degradation of the working self that takes place as a result of unemployment and alienating work. However, the post-Fordist work ethic is more than an ideology, but rather a discursive terrain for the formation of subjectivities through connections between the self and economic value. Experiencing the self as abject to this ethic brings about feelings of devalorization and low self-worth, along with the daily indignities of unemployment and alienated labour. In this sense, while the young people in this chapter are the most cynical about work and the promises of the work ethic, they also experience the harshest consequences of the centrality of the work ethic to subject formation in contemporary capitalism. Their disillusionment with work, their scepticism towards the promises of the work ethic and their reluctance to position themselves in aspirational terms as mandated by the ethic of achievement do not protect them from the experiences of devalorization described so far. They therefore remain compelled to articulate and experience themselves in relation to the moral significance of work, despite the demoralizing experiences they have had in the labour market.

6

Conclusion: Young People in the Work Society

In the work society, the cultivation of the self as a worker is necessary for the experience of a socially intelligible self. It is compulsory both to work and to become a worker – forming the self in line with the disciplinary requirements of labour and experiencing the capacity for productivity as a critical part of personal identity. Becoming economically productive is one of the key tasks of youth, and young people are surrounded by a vast institutional architecture that encourages them to become workers. As shown throughout the previous chapters, young people recognize this as legitimate and necessary, and many understand the successful formation of a working self to be the basic condition for meaning and happiness in life. In responding to the imperative to become a worker, young people demonstrate the profound significance of the post-Fordist work ethic for the formation of youth subjectivities. The post-Fordist work ethic shapes young people's relationship to themselves, their family and friends, educational institutions and jobs. It gives meaning to employment and unemployment, and situates these experiences as part of an autobiographical narrative. The relationship between work and life is mediated by the ethics that drive the cultivation of the self as a worker.

However, young people's practices, subjectivities and definitions of value also complicate contemporary understandings of post-Fordism. The subjectivities that emerge from these practices create questions about epochal distinctions between different eras of capitalism and about the suggestion that work has come to encompass the whole of life. In particular, the relationship between work, value and the self articulates both continuities and disjunctures with earlier manifestations of the work ethic in ways that are classed, and reflect changing distinctions between work and the rest of life. The formation of young people as workers also creates new perspectives on broader issues in the sociology of youth, including in how the nature of youth inequalities are understood and the theoretical and normative frameworks that currently underpin understandings of youth and work. In this concluding chapter, I summarize the project that I have pursued throughout this book and explore the implications of this perspective for understanding young people and contemporary capitalism. The chapter begins by sketching out what is unique about this project and summarizing its findings. It then explores the theoretical implications of understanding youth as subjects of the post-Fordist work ethic, with a focus on theoretical developments in the study of young people and work, broader understandings of post-Fordism and a future agenda for studying youth in post-Fordism.

The formation of young people as workers and the relationship between value and the self

Exploring the formation of young people as workers means examining how the subjectification function of work takes place through young people's practices and relationships to the self. This project sheds a light on what young people do in their lives in order to cultivate themselves as workers, and the relationship with productivity and value that is enacted in these practices. How do young people create working identities, and how does this relate to the way that they understand the capacity for economic productivity as an aspect of themselves? Answering these questions means examining the meanings and investments young people make in work, and the definitions of value and productivity that form part of their understandings of themselves as workers. It means exploring the unique and uniquely powerful promise that the work ethic offers: self-realization through the cultivation of the self as a subject of value to the labour force. In general, much of this book has been dedicated to showing that young people's identities as workers are produced through their commitment to the post-Fordist work ethic as a way of understanding the role of work in their lives. For subjects of the post-Fordist work ethic, the self is realized through the value that it offers to the labour force, and work is approached as a project of self-realization offering unique possibilities for personal fulfilment and satisfaction. However, the way that this takes place is connected with social class, and the classed history of the work ethic means that the post-Fordist work ethic is heterogeneous, allowing different relationships between the self and value that depend on classed identities and experiences of work.

Understanding this means disentangling complex relationships between the self and notions of value that are made invisible by current approaches to youth and work in post-Fordism. In autonomist Marxism (Hardt and Negri, 2004), the self has collapsed entirely into work. Value is produced from all aspects of subjectivity and no aspect of the self is left unproductive. This claim is unsupported by the analysis I have presented throughout this book. The three manifestations of the post-Fordist work ethic that I have explored here enact very different relationships between the self and value. Only one – the ethic of passion – resembles the kind of working subjectivity that collapses the entire self into productivity and value. The other working identities described in Chapters 4 and 5 are based on very different understandings of how the self is mobilized at work. Making these differences explicit is useful for understanding the nature of post-Fordist identities, and the way in which class inequalities interact with the post-Fordist work ethic.

Subjects of passion strive towards the dissolution of the boundary between work and the rest of life, and believe that this is how self-realization through work takes place. As well as investing the entirety of the self into work, subjects of passion see the rest of their lives in terms of value, meaning that the notion of value becomes a part of their life in a uniquely powerful and all-encompassing way. They are of value to the labour force because they add value to everything they do. Everything in life is thereby filtered through the prism of value. Subjects of passion come the closest to the notion that work has become synonymous with life itself. In the ethic of passion, self-realization means realizing a passionate life in general, but passion can be mobilized in a uniquely powerful way at work. Work – as a key signifier of class status and distinction – becomes a focal point for the outpouring of passion, and other aspects of life become significant inasmuch as they furnish passion for work. The cultivation of the self as a worker therefore means harnessing passionate energies across the whole of life and mobilizing these to be successful at work. Subjects of passion are the ideal post-Fordist workers – enthusiastically committed to investing the entirety of themselves at work. They represent the post-Fordist work ethic in its purest form.

Subjects of achievement are formed through an entirely different relationship between work, value and the self – one that does not conform with the suggestion that life is dissolving into work, but does reflect the distinction between work and life in Fordism. For subjects of achievement, the experience of self-realization through work takes place through identifying a discrete aspect of the self that can be cultivated into the capacity for productive labour in an area of the labour market. Subjects of achievement see work as a project of self-realization, but also maintain distinctions between the productive and unproductive dimensions of the self. They do not see the entirety of life as subsumed to value, and continue to articulate the value of work in terms of material security and financial reward. Work continues to serve the rest of life here, as well as operating as a realm for the realization of the self. In this, subjects of achievement demonstrate that arguments about the dissolution of life into work are remote from the experiences and working identities of most young people. Indeed, the capacity and inclination to see the entirety of life as offering value is a form of class privilege that is unavailable to all but those who are used to thinking of themselves as destined for a life of distinction and significance.

What unites the ethic of passion and the ethic of achievement is the notion of work as a realm of authenticity. Approaching work in terms of passion means following a pathway that is unique to yourself, if experienced in terms of a kind of mysterious affective energy. Approaching work in terms of achievement means realizing personal characteristics as valued realms of competence, and therefore finding a place in work that mobilizes these personal traits. For the participants described in Chapter 5, work is not a realm of authentic self-realization but a fraught and risky terrain that is approached in terms of becoming socially appropriate according to rules that always remain somewhat opaque. However, there is a recognition that work matters to the experience of the self in a significant and intimate way, and this recognition motivates efforts to cultivate new aesthetics and interactive styles in the hope that these will be well received on the labour market. This is particularly intense for young women, for whom long-standing notions of respectability and moral value are connected with aesthetic judgements that regulate normative femininity. For workers, the relationship between identity, labour and value is experienced in terms of submitting to alienation and degradation as part of the unfortunate reality of work. This precludes experiencing the self as value, but includes the constant frustration of producing value for others and remaining financially precarious. There is no sense here that life itself is a source for the value of the self as a worker, or that a brighter future awaits those who can more enthusiastically self-realize through work.

The ontological reward of self-realization requires total submission to the post-Fordist work ethic. For subjects of passion, class distinction is made possible by fully and completely investing the self in work and in unreservedly submitting to the disciplinary requirements of work as the basis for the self. They are in this sense the most compliant workers in the labour force. While they experience work as a realm for autonomous self-realization, there is also no aspect of their life that they are not willing to enthusiastically invest in their work and in the value of themselves as workers. The strong sense of personal value that subjects of passion articulate also demonstrates how the post-Fordist work ethic has intertwined selfhood with the logic of value, and the value of the self with the labour force. Those for whom the ontological reward of the work ethic is withheld risk experiencing themselves as valueless, even if their subjectivities are not fully subsumed in work. Even if they are able to work in a way that maintains the rest of their life, the alienation they experience at work and the poor working conditions that this often entails mean that they constantly struggle to salvage a sense of personal value from their working lives. Submission, self-realization and alienation are all part of the heterogeneity of the post-Fordist work ethic in its relation to processes of class distinction.

Attention to young people's actual identity practices and experiences of the working self is critical to understanding the way in which youth subjectivities are produced through the post-Fordist work ethic. These diverse experiences show that while existing theories of post-Fordist identity construction provide an important backdrop to understanding the formation of young people as workers, there are discontinuities in the post-Fordist work ethic that create a more complex picture than the notion of life dissolving into work would allow. The ontological reward of the post-Fordist work ethic is delivered in ways that are intertwined with processes of class distinction that take place through the cultivation of the self as a subject of value to the labour force. The work ethic is also heterogeneous, and the notions of passion and achievement represent historical continuities and ruptures with the Fordist work ethic that make epochal statements about the nature of post-Fordism impossible to sustain. This is especially important given those young people who become abject to the requirements that the work ethic places on them, and for whom the conversion of life into value is remote to their experiences of degradation through unemployment or at work. These differences in the relationship between value and the self are critical both to the post-Fordist work ethic and to the divisions that shape the contemporary youth labour force.

Together, these dynamics begin to sketch what it means to understand the formation of young people as workers. This occurs through practices of self-cultivation that take place within the biopolitical requirements of the post-Fordist work ethic. These requirements are to understand the self in terms of the capacity for economic productivity, and to see the development of this capacity as a process of self-realization and personal fulfilment. Relationships between value and the self also shape the practices through which young people become workers. These practices enact distinctions between work and the rest of life that reflect how young people see their value to the labour force. Youth subjectivities are thereby aligned with the logic of value, which itself is organized as part of the processes of class distinction based on the relationship between value and the self. Through a focus on this relationship in different manifestations of the work ethic, the history of work and identity in capitalism becomes visible in the subjectivities of contemporary young people. Young people who aspire to passionate self-realization echo Weber's notion of work as a vocation, but within a distinctly late modern focus on the self as an end in itself. Aspirations to social mobility resemble the Fordist work ethic, but mobilized within notions of individual aspiration and self-actualization unique to the post-Fordist present. The formation of young people as workers therefore captures how biopolitical practices enact heterogeneous logics of value, which themselves reflect changes in the work ethic in different modes of production.

Post-Fordism and the sociology of youth

One of the key implications of this book is that research perspectives on young people and work must do more to engage with the material and cultural dynamics of contemporary capitalism. Many youth researchers – especially those working from a sociological perspective – may take a focus on capitalism for granted. However, this task is not as straightforward as it may seem given the approaches that are currently shaping work in this field. While the sociology of youth is concerned with a range of aspects of life in capitalist societies, a focus on capitalism as such is marginal to the field (Cote, 2014 and Sukarieh and Tannock, 2014 are two of the notable exceptions to this). The sociology of youth often focuses on various aspects of contemporary capitalism on young people's lives. This includes a long-standing concern with material inequalities among young people, including in their biographical movements through the labour market. Youth unemployment has also long been on the agenda. More recently, a focus on risk and precarity has come to dominate the agenda in studies of youth and work. All of these are aspects of contemporary capitalism. However, a language of capitalism per se as a mode of production that creates subjectivities is largely absent from studies into young people and work.

One outcome of this is that studies of youth and work have failed to critique the assumption that youth should be analysed from the perspective of the supply of labour to capital. This is the perspective taken by social policy regimes that govern youth transitions, in which the aim of institutional interventions into youth is to shepherd young people into whatever work is available. This assumption is left unexamined in research on youth transitions. That young people should become employed is currently taken for granted in youth transitions research, which also assumes that the goal of interventions into young people's working lives should be to support them to do so. Of course, researchers have critically interrogated the normative assumptions that drive these interventions, including the individualistic nature of neoliberal welfare policies and the moralization of inequality that tends to surround these political frameworks. Researchers have also critiqued inequalities in young people's access to good work. However, the basic requirement to form the self as a worker and to contribute to the creation of value remains an unexamined backdrop to critiques of the structural inequalities that impact on young people's capacity to find and retain work.

Rather than taking the necessity of employment transitions for granted, in this book I have made becoming a worker visible as a disciplinary requirement of contemporary valorization regimes. As emphasized in the work of both Weber and Weeks, the work ethic is critical to the creation of a disciplined workforce from subjects who may otherwise be recalcitrant. It is not merely that young people should ideally get jobs, but rather that they are required to become workers, and therefore become subject to the dictates of the work ethic. When they comply with this process, the work ethic allows practices that assign value to young people's subjectivities and connect this to their value to the labour force. In this way, young people's intimate affectivities and social relationships are organized and filtered through the relationship between work, value and the self that the work ethic entails. This process is invisible in existing perspectives, but is nevertheless a necessary outcome of the requirement to work. It is through the work ethic that labour is supplied to capital. The work ethic is therefore not merely a necessity of contemporary capitalism, but a biopolitical regime that must be interrogated for the subjectivities and modes of exploitation that it makes possible. Making this visible raises a range of new questions, including the nature of exploitation in its relationship with youth.

In the sociology of youth as it stands, young people are approached as a highly exploited source of cheap and precarious labour. This exploitation is related to their relatively powerless position in the labour market, state sanctioned wages that are lower than those of adults, and the unserious and stopgap approach to work that young people are supposed to adopt (Tannock, 2001; Mizen, 2004). Young people are thereby exploited to the degree that they work for low wages in poor conditions. In the political economy of youth perspective, this exploitation is also facilitated by the development of false consciousness in young people. For Cote (2014), young people have failed to recognize their objective material interests as a collective of workers owing to an interest in consumption and popular culture, which distracts them from their position as an exploited group and contributes to the profits of the super-rich. If young people became conscious of their status as an exploited group, then they would collectively resist this exploitation. This is basically an orthodox Marxist approach to identity and exploitation, in which youth are regarded as political subjects of capitalism much like the concept of the working class. While this perspective recognizes inequalities among young people that stratify 'youth as a class' (Cote, 2016), these inequalities are unconnected to the definition of exploitation that the political economy of youth perspective introduces to studies of young people and work.

In contrast, in this book I have described three distinct relationships between identity and work and three distinct ways in which exploitation takes place through the formation of young people as workers. Subjects of passion are the most structurally privileged youth, with the highest levels of education and the highest likelihood of secure and high-status work. Subjects of passion are the most confident in their own value and future success. However, they are also those whose experience of themselves is most completely enfolded with their value to the labour force. The exploitation of their labour takes place through the mobilization of their affective energies and intimate lives in ways that go far beyond the notion of false consciousness. Their hobbies, friendships and private moments of relaxation are all mobilized in the cultivation of a working identity, and are therefore all exploitable aspects of their subjectivities. However, subjects of passion also receive the highest rewards both inside and outside work. Their commitment to the exploitation of their labour is rewarded with high status, financial compensation and feelings of pleasure and self-realization through the attribution of value to themselves and others. It is only within the ethic of passion that the promises of the post-Fordist work ethic work ethic are properly fulfilled, meaning that while passionate subjects are formed through regimes of exploitation, they are also given enormously expansive rewards. This is the ontological reward of exploitation within the post-Fordist work ethic.

Together with subjects of passion, subjects of achievement represent a mode of exploitation that takes place through striving for authenticity rather than accepting alienation. Subjects of achievement aim to realize themselves authentically through competence and achievement. They are exploited through their aspirations for social mobility and by their desire to avoid what they see as the disaster of alienated labour. They pursue the ontological reward of the work ethic just as enthusiastically as subjects of passion. However, they are motivated as much by anxiety about failure as by belief in their own value. Their energetic adherence to the work ethic reflects their aspiration to be fully realized as competent and valued

130

workers, but does not include a total investment of their intimate and affective lives in the way described by passionate workers. The rewards of the work ethic include supporting the remainder of life as well as realizing the self at work. They maintain a desire for social mobility motivated by a mixture of aspiration and anxiety. This deep investment in accruing value to the self and avoiding the disaster of failure makes subjects of achievement into exploitable workers even as they recognize that there is life outside work. These fears and anxieties are what define the formation of young people as workers according to the ethic of achievement. This experience also emphasizes the heterogeneous nature of the post-Fordist work ethic and the modes of exploitation it facilitates, both in terms of definitions of value and the relationship between value and the self.

Young people who struggle to create socially appropriate and credentialled working identities are exploited in their experience of alienation at work and in their exclusion from the ontological reward of the work ethic. They accept that work is likely to be unpleasant and degrading, but its material necessity means they also aim to prepare the image of a well-disciplined worker in order to secure employment. This includes working on their personal affectivities and relational styles, although not with the aim of authentic self-realization but rather in an attempt to adhere to the opaque rules that govern which identities are included and excluded at work. The main reward of work is therefore to sustain their lives with a minimum of fuss and degradation, and good work means a stable income with a minimum of interference in the rest of life. Despite accepting the alienation of work, these young people also recognize the significance of work for the experience of personal value and as a basis for recognition as a socially intelligible subject. However, they cannot relate to this in terms of authenticity but rather in terms of 'getting it right', and therefore being recognized as valued by employers and the welfare agencies that frequently intervene in their lives. This struggle for appropriate self-presentation is part of the experience of alienation in the context of the post-Fordist work ethic, as well as the precarious and degrading experience of unemployment and low-wage service work. Rather than being exempt from the disciplinary requirements of the work ethic, these young people are abject to the labouring subjectivities made available to more privileged youth.

Different relationships between the self and value therefore lead to different modes of exploitation, all of which are part of the post-Fordist work ethic. In acknowledging this heterogeneity, we are at some distance from the notion of false consciousness. It is not merely that young people are blind to their material interests, but rather that work and value are the key terrain on which youth subjectivities are formed. Comparing their identities as workers to a possible revolutionary consciousness makes this process invisible, and therefore obscures the significance of the work ethic for both young people and contemporary capitalism. Moreover, exploitation does not take place merely through poor wages and working conditions. Instead, exploitation is a condition for the formation of youth subjectivities in general. In becoming intertwined with the imperative for authenticity and self-realization, exploitation reaches into the private moments of young people's lives, and impacts upon everything from their leisure pursuits to the bodily gestures through which they present themselves to the world. Privileged young people are in many ways those most compliant to the work ethic, although they also receive the highest rewards. Those whose lives are positioned as valueless by the work ethic are also those who perform the most precarious and alienated labour, and who experience the most profound degradation through unemployment and at work. Exploitation therefore takes place through a complex and ambivalent set of relationships between value and the self that are connected with social class and lead to qualitatively different experiences of work and life in general. This is how youth is exploited through the formation of the working self.

By organizing labouring subjectivities and modes of exploitation, the post-Fordist work ethic creates and regulates the youth labour force. In the sociology of youth, it has become common to understand the youth labour market as precarious and risky because of labour market deregulation driven by neoliberal employment policies. However, the formation of young people as workers is regulated by the work ethic, which shapes the relationship that young people must take to themselves and to work. The ethic of self-realization results in a labour force that is highly invested in offering value to employers and is regulated through young people's intimate desires for happiness and fulfilment in life. In this, the post-Fordist work ethic makes enormous demands on young people. They are expected to cultivate themselves as workers throughout much of their lives, and they respond to this expectation in a highly disciplined manner. The outcome is a youth labour force that is – following authors working in the governmentality tradition – governed through the mobilization and regulation of the 'soul' (Rose, 1999) and its investment in work. For young people themselves, self-government through self-actualization is also a meaningful ethic to navigate labour market uncertainty. Processes of self-actualization are seen to reflect the value of the self, and risky labour markets can be navigated by cultivating this value. By focusing on young people's practices and working subjectivities, the youth labour force emerges as a highly regulated biopolitical terrain formed through the requirement to cultivate and attribute value to the self.

These processes become visible only when the relationship between youth and work is understood as part of post-Fordist capitalism. The key processes here are labour force formation, exploitation and the relationship between value and the self that is produced through contemporary regimes of production and valorization. In this book, I have shown how youth subjectivities are created through the requirement to become workers within a work ethic that reflects these valorization regimes. Existing concerns in the sociology of youth, such as biographical inequalities, labour market precarity and unemployment, are all part of these broader political and economic relations and should be situated as such. Without this theorization, studies of youth and work are abstracted from the dynamics of post-Fordist capitalism, and the field risks contributing to agendas that are aimed more at providing labour to capital than at arriving at a critical understanding of work and life.

Young people and class inequality

Across a range of important publications, Skeggs has approached social class in terms of enactments and contestations of notions of value (Skeggs, 1997, 2004, 2005, 2011). For Skeggs, class is embodied through the imposition of notions of value onto the self, including the moralization of value in terms of values for judging others. Skeggs also draws attention to mobilizations and resistances to the value form as a way of thinking about the self and social life. These mobilizations of value and values are key to the way in which the post-Fordist work ethic operates in the lives of young people and suggests two key shifts in studies of young people and class. The first is to move away from a focus on the exchange of resources for wages on the labour market. The second is to develop notions such as distinction and symbolic value through situating them as aspects of identity and value within post-Fordism. These approaches to inequality underpin the transitions and Bourdieusian perspectives respectively. As discussed in Chapter 2, the transitions approach to youth is based on what Lisa Adkins (2005b) has described as the social contract view of work, in which the employment relation consists of the production of value through the exchange of resources for wages. The social contract approach understands work as a realm that is separate from the rest of social life and is negotiated as such in order to secure employment. This is basically the premise of studies of youth transitions, in which biographical inequalities emerge from an interaction between socially distributed resources and labour market structures. Inequalities are understood in terms of levels of remuneration, managerial status, precarity and overall autonomy over working conditions. Social class is therefore created through the exchange of unequally distributed resources for wages and job security. The formation of young people as workers implies a different approach to social class – one premised on the cultivation and attribution of value and the relationship between value and the self. In the formation of young people as workers, class is approached in terms of the relationship between notions of value reflecting classed history of the work ethic, enacted through the biopolitical practices of post-Fordist labour force formation. This is what it means to shift from studying youth transitions to the subjectification function of work.

Understanding this process requires some revision of Bourdieu's concept of distinction. In his work, classed subjectivities emerge through the pursuit of symbolic capital. This takes place according to historically embedded dispositions (the habitus) that shape how subjects accumulate capital. The habitus creates perceptions of meaning and possibility and shapes the practices that classed subjects use to pursue symbolic capital according to these perceptions. Because symbolic distinctions are connected with material conditions, class distinction is based around the 'distance from necessity' that subjects can achieve. The highest levels of distinction are conferred upon those who can position themselves as most elevated in relation to the necessities of material survival, and symbolic capital is also defined in terms of this distance from necessity (Bourdieu, 1990). Adkins (2005b) has critiqued the notion of capitals as connected to a social contract view of labour in which subjects are regarded as 'owning' capital, which is then alienated from them in the employment relation. For this reason, Adkins suggests that the concept of the ownership of capital cannot capture the relationship between value and the self in post-Fordism. In one sense, this critique can be seen as unfair, since for Bourdieu the habitus and symbolic capital are connected (for example, in the notion of embodied capitals) and thus not necessarily based on this relation of ownership. Nevertheless, Adkins's critique raises an important problem for understanding class at work. While Bourdieu's influence has placed the cultural politics of identity at the centre of class analysis, critiques such as that of Adkins are an important reminder of situating subjectivity and value within the specific forms of labouring subjectivity demanded of workers in post-Fordism. Rather than hierarchies of symbolic value, class at work is connected to the capacities required to produce economic value.

By analysing distinction as organized around different approaches to economic productivity, in this book I have tried to show how the formation of young people as workers operates as a site for the negotiation of value and values. The relationship between productivity and subjectivity in general varies both historically and within contemporary class relations in ways that are specific to the social organization of work. In particular, I have shown that distance from necessity is achieved through a passionate investment in the dictates of the post-Fordist work ethic. In a sense this is ironic, since it describes a situation in which distance from material necessity is cultivated through a total commitment to becoming economically productive. This commitment includes all aspects of the self, and so passionate commitment is in this respect most closely aligned with the logic of work. However, the cultivation of distinction through a passionate commitment to work is made possible by the ontological reward offered by the post-Fordist work ethic, which positions work as a realm whose significance lies beyond material necessity. Distance from necessity is therefore built into the post-Fordist work ethic. It is critical to receiving the ontological reward of selfhood through work. Through the ethic of passion, all aspects of a worker's subjectivity are elevated beyond the material realm, and value is positioned as the only significant basis for a socially intelligible self. By situating productivity as passionate self-realization, the ethic of passion celebrates the value form as the basis for the self in general.

There are echoes of Bourdieusian distinction throughout the definitions of value enacted throughout this book, although this is cultivated and mobilized in ways that are specific to the post-Fordist work ethic. In particular, the ethic of achievement shows how working-class identities become intertwined with the logic of value through the moralization of social mobility as a compulsory aspiration as they are manifested in the work ethic. The ethic of achievement mobilizes notions of productivity, value and the self that characterized working-class relationships to work in Fordism, but within notions of self-realization and distinction that are specific to the post-Fordist present. Moreover, the ethic of achievement is closer to necessity than the ethic of passion. Self-realization through competence and achievement is the ontological reward for escaping a life of drudgery and financial hardship. The risk of falling into precarity and disadvantage is narrated alongside the loss of value, uniqueness and pride in the self that this would entail. The resentments and anxieties articulated by subjects of achievement are also discussed in Bourdieu's (1984) account of aspirations to social mobility, but in the contemporary context reflect the pressure on young people to form themselves as aspirational subjects through work. In this sense, the ethic of achievement reflects the transformation of working-class identities through the relationship between class, value and the work ethic amid the precarity and structural uncertainty of post-Fordist labour markets.

While Skeggs has argued that working-class subjectivities are enacted through resisting the value form as the basis for the self, the formation of young people as workers produces experiences of exclusion and symbolic violence through the definitions of value at the heart of the post-Fordist work ethic. In regarding work as an alien and unfamiliar realm requiring studied and careful self-presentation, the cultivation of a credentialled and socially appropriate self enacts processes of symbolic violence, such as those initially described by Bourdieu. For Bourdieu, exclusion is understood in terms of lacking the dispositions required to understand the 'rules of the game' and comport the self accordingly. For the marginalized, efforts to adhere to these rules are necessarily forced and contrived – deliberately cultivated rather than authentically expressed. This lack of effortless authenticity reinscribes the marginalization of those who are marginalized in advance – marking them as failures within the game being played. However, symbolic violence also differs in important ways when it takes place through the formation of the working self and when it is connected to the post-Fordist work ethic. When the reward for becoming a worker is ontological rather than material, it is not possible to make a virtue of one's exclusion. The post-Fordist work ethic amplifies and generalizes the critical significance of work for the social intelligibility of the self while aligning selfhood with the logic of value. This means that experiences of unemployment create the sense that one is unable to 'get it right' because of something deeply wrong with the self. This is a form of all-encompassing devalorization that leaves no space for virtue in exclusion. Compounded by material impoverishment, this is the experience of abjection and symbolic violence produced through unemployment and alienated labour in post-Fordism.

In summary, class inequalities are manifested not merely in the exchange of resources or in the struggle for symbolic value, but in the classed history of the work ethic as a cultural formation that shapes the organization of labour and the relationship between value and the self. Class distinctions differentiate the ethical commitments that young people make to work, the relationship to value and productivity that these ethics entail, and the meaning attributed to money and social status. It is the history of class that makes the work ethic heterogeneous. The fullest realization of the post-Fordist work ethic aligns with middle-class modes of distinction, but also shapes aspirations and experiences of symbolic violence for those who are excluded in advance from the total dissolution of the self into work. Classed subjectivities are therefore organized around the relationship between the self and value, and in the modes of economic selfhood that are valorized and devalorized through this relation. The practices that young people mobilize in order to become productive are premised on this relationship, which itself reflects shifts in the meaning of work in different eras of capitalism. This is how classed divisions in the youth labour force emerge through the cultivation of the self as a worker.

Conclusion

Understanding the formation of the self as a worker shifts the nature of youth as an object of study. Youth is transformed from a process of resource accumulation to a biopolitical relationship between the self, productivity and value. It is not merely that young people require the resources to engage with work, but rather that youth itself is a product of the disciplinary requirements of work. Within this framework, youth subjectivities emerge as a series of productive capacities created and mobilized through the mandate to achieve self-realization. These capacities are distributed through the heterogeneity of the post-Fordist work ethic in its relationship to class distinction. The post-Fordist work ethic organizes the relationship between work and life at the level of youth subjectivities and situates work as basic to the value of the self. This relationship is fundamental to the position of young people as workers within post-Fordist capitalism. The work ethic is critical to both the formation of the youth labour force and to young people's orientations to the rest of their lives. In this sense, studying the relationship between young people and work means exploring how distinction, exploitation and productivity are intertwined in the creation of youth subjectivities. This is the kind of agenda that I would like to encourage through this book in the sociology of youth. To conclude, I want to suggest three future directions that follow from the agenda as outlined here. These are designed to analyse the specific industrial and institutional contexts as well as political relationships through which the work ethic is articulated and contested by young people.

The first is to reframe the significance of education and the role of education in the creation of workers. Gerrard's recent discussion of the learning ethic (Gerrard, 2014) describes how notions of lifelong learning have become intertwined with the work ethic. Gerrard argues that the necessity of cultivating a productive self has become connected to new discourses of education, which mandate a constant and flexible accumulation of new skills. In this book, I have shown that young workers' approach to education and to knowledge varies according to the ethic through which they approach self-realization. Education for the young people in this book is about realizing passion, cultivating competence or accumulating credentials. Each of these relationships to education is part of a different manifestation of the work ethic While the connection between educational qualifications and labour market trajectories has become increasingly uncertain (Chesters et al, 2018), the post-Fordist work ethic articulates connections between education and work on the level of young people's biographies in ways that vary according to the ethics of self-realization pursued by differently positioned youth. In this context, this book suggests that the post-Fordist work ethic may be contributing to the relationship between education and class in ways that have implications for the creation of student identities and notions of employability as they are experienced by students and mobilized in governmental interventions into the labour market.

The second avenue of future research is to understand how the projects of self-realization described in this book are connected with the labour processes of specific industries. This book has remained within the long-standing tradition in the sociology of youth of focusing on young people's biographical narratives, and analysing how different social and institutional contexts are drawn into these narratives in the articulation of subject positions. It is not therefore a book about labour as such, but about the cultivation of the working self. However, this process is likely to take place in unique ways within different industrial contexts, which vary enormously in terms of the organizational structures that shape the demands placed upon young people. The contemporary world of work consists of an increasing proliferation of such structures, including traditional professional hierarchies, contemporary 'flat' and 'flexible' organizations, modes of work resembling both self-employment and precarious waged work (such as the 'gig economy') and forms of employment such as interactive service labour, which place enormous demands on young people's subjectivities while remaining precarious and poorly remunerated. These are likely to interact in complex ways with young people's understandings of themselves as productive workers, especially as they gain more experience in the labour market. Examining this interaction is important for understanding how productive capacities are formed in industrial context as well as through biographical practices.

The third and final future direction is to examine how young people's identities as workers interact with their political relationship to work. In a sense, the arguments I have presented here are politically pessimistic, depicting young people who are optimistically invested in a fantasy of self-realization through labour that amounts to a full and uncritical investment in their own exploitation. Their narratives are also highly individualistic, and suited more to negotiating precarity than challenging it. However, for the vast majority of young people it is unlikely that the vast promises of the work ethic will be realized. Their investments are at odds with the material reality of the youth labour market, in which precarity, unemployment and underemployment are now the norm. Those young people who are excluded from the subjectivities valorized by the work ethic have experienced this first hand. In this context, what forms of political resistance or new political possibilities are available to post-Fordist subjects for whom work is both precarious and necessary for social intelligibility? How might different relationships between value and the self facilitate new relations between employment and citizenship amid the decline of formal unionized politics? These are the kinds of questions that I hope to have made possible in the future by opening up the formation of young people as workers as an object of research.

Methodological Afterword

This final section of the book is aimed at those readers who are interested in the methodological processes that led to the three-part analysis I have presented in this book. To some, dividing the post-Fordist work ethic into three categories or types may appear anachronistic. After all, sociologists are increasingly being encouraged to attend to 'mess' in social scientific research (Law, 2004). We are encouraged to write about the world in ways that are non-linear and that emphasize the complexity and non-linearity of social relationships. By dividing the work ethic into three ideal types, perhaps I am at risk of reducing the social production and contestation of identity into a series of reified categories, and rendering the social world as both simpler and more deterministic than is actually the case. In this afterword I want to anticipate and address these critiques in a way that is both methodologically reflexive and that supports the analysis I have presented throughout the book.

The afterword is organized in two sections. The first provides an account of the analytical process that led to the creation of these categories. This includes a discussion of Max Weber's original ideas on the creation of 'ideal types' that inspired the analysis here, and an explanation of how Weber's methods shaped the book's analysis. However, in the second section I want to invite critical attention to these categories through the experiences of a participant whose identity as a worker lies somewhere between the ethics of passion and achievement, and whose experience of substantial social mobility may test the limits of my framework. The ultimate argument I want to make here is that the approach I have developed in this book inspired by Weber's methods has value inasmuch as it emphasizes and creates conceptual relationships between aspects of the self at work that have become critical in post-Fordism. In this, it necessarily imposes a conceptual logic on a world that does not follow the same rules as theory, but in doing so provides an important insight even into experiences that may not immediately appear to follow the conceptual logic of the book.

Ideal types and the post-Fordist work ethic

The concept of 'ideal types' is most famously articulated in Weber's essay titled 'Objectivity' in Social Science and Social Policy (Weber, 1949), and is known to most undergraduate students studying the social sciences. Weber's methodological work inspired an enormous literature that I cannot review exhaustively here, but has a few key characteristics that have been useful for my analysis in this book and can assist others in evaluating the methods that I have used. For Weber, ideal types are a way of ordering empirical reality according to the features that are most significant for the purposes of the analyst. They are a 'mental construct for the scrutiny and systematic characterization of individual concrete patterns' (Weber, 1949, p 100). Weber emphasizes that ideal types are a way of rendering down the limitless complexity of day-to-day social life into a series of elements or phenomena that can be used to build theory. An ideal type is constructed by accentuating a few characteristics of a type of phenomenon, and then creating a concept out of these features. While necessarily shaped by the values and interests of socially situated researchers (a critical concern for Weber), this is an empirically driven process:

> [an ideal type's] relationship to the empirical data consists solely in the fact that where ... relationships of the type referred to by the abstract construct are discovered or suspected to exist in reality to some extent, we can make the *characteristic* features of this relationship pragmatically *clear* and *understandable* by reference to an *ideal-type* ... An ideal type is formed by the one-sided accentuation of one or more point of view and by the synthesis of a great many diffuse, discrete, more or less present and occasionally absent concrete individual phenomena, which are arranged according to those one-sidedly emphasised viewpoints into a unified analytical construct. (Weber, 1949, p 90, emphasis in original)

While creating ideal types is an empirically driven process, they are not just descriptions of reality, but offer a means to express the nature of social life with a view to building theory (Weber, 1949, p 90; see also Rosenberg, 2015). Ideal types necessarily impose a sense of abstract logic on a messy world in order to render the world amenable to being understood sociologically. In this sense, Weber describes ideal types as 'utopias', where the world operates with a logic and rationality that is defined as such by accentuating what is critical for the analyst and what is most theoretically salient for a project. For example, Weber's notion of the

'Protestant ethic' is created by emphasizing those aspects of Protestantism that are relevant to economic life. While Weber emphasizes that religious ideas have an almost infinite complexity in lived experience, the Protestant ethic is identified through accentuating those aspects of Protestantism that are visibly mobilized in disciplining the working class. Protestantism is thereby rendered as an ideal type in order to arrive at an explanation of class formation and the emergence of capitalism.

Weber's concept of ideal types is also a way of accounting methodologically for the role of theory and researcher positionality in framing what counts as significant in a research project. Weber's objectivity essay repeatedly emphasizes the infinite complexity of the social world and the limitless connections to be made between one aspect of social life and another. In this context, Weber is clear that sociological researchers do not create perfect reflections of society. Instead, researchers create explanations by systematically slicing the world into significant elements and identifying connections between these elements. In this way, ideal types can be created, providing insight into an aspect of the social world that is rendered interesting according to the priorities of a researcher. This necessarily takes place by abstracting ideal types from the 'mess' of social life.

However, Weber is also aware and critical of the risk of reification – that is, of attributing a material reality to abstract concepts, and then approaching the world as though the abstract concepts of the researcher themselves shape actual social practices. This is especially significant for Weber given the intellectual currents of his time. Weber is critical of both naturalistic positivism and positivistic interpretations of Marxism owing to their reliance on reified notions of causal laws. While these approaches considered an analysis complete if it could be extrapolated from these laws, Weber emphasizes that social phenomena should be analysed in their historical contingency, and that extrapolation from laws mistakes theoretical explanation for the world being explained. This is also a concern for Bourdieu (1990), for whom Weber is a major inspiration. For both Weber and Bourdieu, sociology necessarily imposes an abstract logic on the world in order to create meaningful explanations and useful theory, but must avoid approaching the world as though it operates according to a theoretical logic. In articulating the concept of ideal types, Weber constantly makes a differentiation between the world of theory and the world as it is experienced by social actors, while at the same time emphasizing the necessity of conceptual abstraction to generate adequate explanations for social life. Ideal types do not determine actions and thoughts: they are a way of expressing these in a way that creates theory. Consistent with his critique of positivism, ideal types for Weber are not 'laws' but concepts that are evaluated in terms of their adequacy in characterizing a particular part of social life understood in its uniqueness. The concept of ideal types therefore makes the abstraction at the heart of social research methods explicit, while at the same time emphasizing the necessary gap between the world of intellectual ideas and day-to-day social life.

The Protestant ethic offers an example of this process. Weber shows how an effortful commitment to work as the pathway to salvation was made consistent with the notion of predestination, in which the saved were chosen in advance. Viewing this as a contradiction would impose the logic of theory on the world of lived experience, whereas for Weber the logic of this ethic is analysed in its uniqueness and used to create the concept of the Protestant ethic. What matters for Weber's analysis is not subjecting the Protestant ethic to a test of logical consistency, but creating conceptually meaningful conceptions between this concept and capitalism. For this reason, the apparent contradiction between predestination and salvation through work is less important than the way in which the Protestant emphasis on displays of success as a reflection of chosen status contributes to class formation in capitalism. Like the work of Bourdieu, Weber's approach to ideal types is therefore situated within an account of the social world that emphasizes tension, and explores how people are collectively oriented towards one another despite living with tension and contradiction in their day-to-day social lives. This is made possible through the logic of theory, which creates conceptual consistency from lived contradiction.

While I did not initially intend to use this approach in this book, the process of coding and recoding familiar to all qualitative researchers led me back to Weber's ideas as a useful way of approaching patterns that were emerging in the way that young people talked about the meaning of work. I began the project interested in how young people were relating to work, and approached the data in the context of theoretical arguments about the collapse of work into the self. It soon became clear that the relationship between work and the self varied in significant ways for differently positioned young people. However, this variation could be understood in terms of a small number of critical issues and attributions of meaning. I therefore constructed the three manifestations of the work ethic described in this book with Weber's advice in mind. I have aimed to identify and emphasize what is most significant in the contingency and uniqueness of young people's approach to work in order to contribute to theories of post-Fordism and of the relationship between youth and work. In this, I have theorized the work ethic as having a conceptual logic, despite the contradictions it creates in young people's lives and despite the inevitable messiness of their actual experiences of work now and in the future. The conceptual logic of the work ethic is created by limiting my focus to three issues: the aspects of the self that are understood as economically productive, the practices that are deployed to cultivate these productive capacities, and the relationship between value and the self that is enacted in these practices.

These are the lynchpins of the work ethic. The conceptual distinctions I have made in this book (reflected in the organization of the empirical chapters) are based on different manifestations of these three relationships. By narrowing focus in this way, I have been able to apply empirical scrutiny to concepts such as post-Fordism, and create ideal typical concepts that can be brought together into a theoretical approach to the formation of young people as workers. These distinctions necessarily impose order on a world that is messier than the creation of categories would allow. However, these are not simply categories but ideal types – concepts built through emphasizing and focusing on the aspects of young people's narratives that are most characteristic of their approach to work. In this sense, their aim is not merely to describe young people's experiences (although they also do this), but to identify and accentuate characteristics of their working identities that can be examined in relation to one another in order to build theory. I am not simply suggesting that the youth labour market contains three types of worker as though this exhaustively catalogues all of the orientations to work that are available to young people. But I am suggesting that these three ideal typical manifestations of the work ethic enact different relationships between economic productivity, the cultivation of the self and the notion of value, and that differences in these relationships provide an important insight into the creation of working identities in post-Fordist capitalism (itself an ideal type). These types are a way of setting an agenda that can be critiqued and developed in future research.

An example of a productive separation between the logic of theory and that of the common-sense world is the way that in the ethic of passion, distance from necessity is achieved through a full investment in work. In a sense, this could be seen as a contradiction at the level of lived experience since it entails a full commitment to material productivity. Indeed, this contradiction is present in the narratives of subjects of passion. They are entirely comfortable attributing a rather expansive significance to their work, but dance around the issue of remuneration in a way that demonstrates the uncomfortable closeness between work and necessity in a society where work is the basis for material survival. However, understanding the ethic of passion as an ideal type means that this contradiction at the level of experience can be abstracted and, within the framework of the book, understood in terms of a connection between productivity, identity and social class. These connections are made consistent through their relationship with the ontological reward of the work ethic. The contradiction faced by research participants is instructive for building the concept of the ethic of passion, but does not lead to a contradiction at the level of the ideal type, because the logic of this concept is to theorize the relationship between the post-Fordist work ethic and class on a conceptual level. Conversely, resolving the contradiction between distance from necessity and the material necessity of work is unlikely to be a priority for participants in their lives, because day-to-day social life is not logically coherent in the way that theory should be. Making sense of this contradiction is necessary for the framework of the book, but this takes place conceptually and not in the empirical world, because the concerns of theory are not the concerns of our participants. This separation is necessary for avoiding reification.

In this book, I have deliberately offered a 'tidy' analysis, at least in relation to the mess and ambiguity of day-to-day social life. Like Weber, my aim here has been to emphasize what is most conceptually significant about the world, while being explicit about the aims of the project (which are driven by theories of post-Fordism) and about the analytical process that I have described in this afterword. The tidiness and restricted parameters of the analysis is a deliberate methodological decision and is arguably necessary for building good theory. However, in the next section I want to explore the experiences of a participant whose biography and attitudes towards work transgress the ideal typical distinctions of the book. This ambivalence is instructive for the value that an ideal typical analysis offers to understanding the work ethic. This example provides an opportunity for methodological reflexivity and invites critique from those who anticipate more 'mess' in contemporary sociological analysis.

Between the ethics

In this section, I focus on two interviews I conducted with a participant I will call Amy. Amy is a junior accountant whom I met through Meg. Meg features in Chapter 3 as a deeply passionate worker. Since they are both accountants, Amy's day-to-day working life is similar to Meg's in many respects. However, unlike Meg, whose parents also had a history of professional employment and tertiary education, Amy has experienced substantial social mobility throughout her working life. Amy left home at the age of 16 and worked in retail while supporting herself through the remainder of her schooling. She did well at school and made it into university, where she studied accounting. Her reason for this choice was that accounting capitalized on her abilities in mathematics and problem-solving, but was also obviously vocational: by studying accounting, she could become an accountant:

> 'How did you end up doing this?'
> 'Well, accounting was my best subject [at school]. I think it was because I didn't have any security. I wanted something that was secure and I was OK at it, so I just did it.
> 'I think it was just because I had this goal. I like it. I like my job and I've always liked problem-solving. I used to get my mum to write out sums for me when I was 5. I like problem-solving. It's weird that when something doesn't balance, I thrive on it. I will sit there for hours until I can get it to balance, and it frustrates me but it makes me feel good at the same time. So I actually like it.'

So far, Amy fits perfectly into the ideal typical characterization of subjects of achievement, who cultivate long-standing interests or capacities into skills, but with an eye to vocational opportunities.

After finishing her degree, Amy found a job in a local accountancy firm where she was working when I interviewed her in 2016 and again 2017. However, Amy felt out of place in this firm. She had different values to her colleagues, whom she characterized as socially and politically conservative as opposed to sharing her progressive views on family, marriage and issues such as migration and refugees, which were points of public debate in Australia during the time of the study. Overall, Amy felt that while there were some parts of her that fitted her job, there were other parts that were deeply at odds with her work (which at one point she described as 'helping rich people not pay tax'). This caused her some anxiety, and she reflected on it throughout the interview in response to questions:

> 'Do you feel like accountancy really clicks with who you are?'
> 'No.'
> 'Really? Not at all?'
> 'No. I think an ideal job would be like a florist or something. Very low stress.'
> 'Why do you think you've ended up working somewhere where everyone is so different to you?'
> 'There's a part of me that must be analytical, but then there's a big part of me that's not. I could work with children or

something. That's the kind of thing that I feel like would be suited to my personality.'

Amy felt deeply conflicted about her working life – proud of her achievements but uncomfortable with the distance she felt from her colleagues. This had been noticed by her friend Meg, whom she had met at university. Meg and Amy met regularly and talked about work and life in general. During these discussions, Meg started to give Amy advice on how she could start to be 'more authentic' at work – advice that Amy was eager to hear since she hoped it would make her happier in the success she had achieved. Through this friendship, Amy heard about leadership training programmes for young professionals, and became motivated to get involved:

> 'I've signed up to do this leadership thing and it's with refugees … You just have to mentor them for three months, I think. I have to go to their information night on Friday. There's also an Australian Business Week thing with the local school that I went to. They do it every year down the road and it goes through this planning of a motel and stuff. They were looking for mentors for that so I'm going to do that as well. So I'm just trying to get involved in things. I feel like that's the only way that I'm going to grow myself.'

Amy is starting to sound more like a subject of passion here. Personal growth and an involvement in local community activities becomes a way of cultivating herself as a worker. Leadership training motivated by an investment in a kind of cosmopolitanism is positioned on the pathway to authenticity at work. However, this was not a straightforward process. Despite her relationship with Meg, Amy's experience of social mobility also resembles the tensions experienced by subjects of achievement in distancing her from her social origins. This distancing has ambivalent consequences for Amy, who is proud of her achievements while feeling uncomfortable with the concept of herself as a high-status worker:

> 'Like if someone says, "What do you do?" and I say, "I'm an accountant", they're like, "Oh wow. Really?" and it's just this label that you have. But I don't think it's a big deal. My friends and my sister that I live with, they haven't gone to uni and they always get really upset if I talk about uni because they didn't go, like I think I'm better because I went to uni. But I actually think uni was a bit of a joke because I didn't learn anything I

needed to know ... It's probably just because not a lot of the people that I surround myself with have a kind of status job. But I don't look at it as any different ... I'm obviously proud of myself for doing it but I avoid talking about it.'

Here, Amy articulates pride in her achievements, as well as feeling uncomfortable at the idea that she is 'better' than others owing to her education. Her degree does not have a strong place in her overall narrative of becoming a worker, but this is because she found that the skills she learned at university did not help her much with the duties of her job (rather than because skills are less relevant than passion, as is the case for passionate subjects). At the same time, Amy is aware that she has a 'status job', at least in relation to her friends and family who are stuck in the low-wage service economy. She is happy with this status, but unwilling to leave her friends and family behind.

When I interviewed her a second time, Amy had had what she called 'life coaching sessions' with Meg. While she had been promoted at work and had received a substantial increase in her pay, she was still critical of her workplace culture and still did not feel as if she belonged. Discussing these themes, Amy returned to her motivations for going to university and working towards a 'status job', despite the difficulties of supporting herself through her education and the social distance it created between herself and her friends:

'Things were said about me, that I was just nothing, so I'm trying to be the opposite of that. So I never go home and just watch TV. Mum, aunties, nan, comments like that. So I've tried to be nothing like them, and be better. So that's why I'm different, because my drive is probably not authentic. So I'm putting things on my plate that are making me this person that I have in my head that I want to be, but that person is not what I wanna be, I wanna be this other person, but I have to prove that I can do this stuff. so that's why I don't really care about achievements, because it's not my passion. it's just more of a – I think that's why everything's conflicted. Cos it's not – yeah.'

As she says in this quote, Amy is deeply conflicted about the course her life has taken. She is motivated to escape becoming 'nothing', which she says reflects frustration at the low expectations for her life that her family expressed when she was younger. Her university degree and professional job are substantial achievements and she has successfully proved her family wrong. However, she sees her achievements as 'inauthentic' and does not feel that the social position granted to her by these achievements reflects who she really is. Importantly, Amy does not feel any imposter syndrome. She was frustrated with her co-workers' sense of comfortable privilege, but had a low opinion of their skills and capabilities and did not feel any less deserving of her success than they were. Instead, Amy's feeling of discomfort comes from what she describes as the misalignment between her work and her passion. Amy does not have a sense of where her passion will take her, but she knows that it is not realized in her achievements at work. She is reflecting on her life, and in her conversations with Meg is working towards discovering how she might discover and realize where her passions lie.

Amy occupies a space in between the different manifestations of the work ethic, entirely fitting neither ideal type but resembling both achievement and passion in her practices and experiences. As she says in the quote, she is invested in being authentic at work but the person she wants to be is not the person she wants to be. The ethic of achievement has not entirely delivered on its promises, but the ethic of passion requires a level of easy privilege that is at odds with her background, experiences and values. The practices that she has drawn upon in cultivating a working identity resemble those of subjects of achievement, including educational pathways that develop long-standing competencies into vocational skills. The value she places on material security and the pride she articulates in having achieved her goals are also important aspects of the ethic of achievement. However, Amy experiences a sense of discomfort with her eventual work that comes from the feeling that her identity is not fully realized at work. This is undoubtedly a consequence of her social mobility, which is often manifested in a feeling of being 'out of place' even if she does not necessarily feel undeserving. Amy is uncomfortable with the distinction conferred through her job, but her feelings of frustration primarily reflect feelings of deep ambivalence about her day-to-day working life – her duties and colleagues. This experience finds expression in the language of passion, which emerges in her second interview after her life coaching with Meg. Amy wants a job where she can realize her broader ethical commitments, but unlike many subjects of passion she does not feel entitled to see this in everything she does. Instead, Amy is reflecting on where her passions may take her, and is cultivating passion (for instance through community leadership activities) in the hope that this will guide her along a more fulfilling pathway through work.

Amy does not fit comfortably into the ideal typical concepts developed in this book. In this sense, she demonstrates the limits of an ideal typical analysis for capturing the complexity that many working subjects feel about their work and their life, and I have included her experiences in this afterword as a way of stimulating critique of my argument. However, Amy's experience also demonstrates why building concepts on the basis of ideal types is useful. Situating her experiences between the ethics of passion and achievement lend a conceptual logic to a life characterized by profound ambivalence. Incorporating elements of both passion and achievement, Amy's experiences are a unique example of contradictions produced through social mobility, class distinction and efforts to realize the self at work. The sense of personal crisis she articulates in interviews demonstrates what happens when the promises of the work ethic are not forthcoming. In this, Amy is grappling with the competing logics of self-formation that make up the post-Fordist work ethic as theorized in this book. While she is between the concepts developed in previous chapters, her narrative is nevertheless organized around the critical issues I have raised throughout this book, especially the relationship between the productive capacities of the self, notions of personal authenticity and class distinction, all of which are at stake in her search for the self-realization that work offers. These aspects of her narrative become visible having been raised and theorized by the conceptual framework developed in this book, and I invite critique and further development of this framework.

Conclusion

Ideal typical analysis creates a conceptual logic from a messy and indeterminate world. The aim of this book has been to highlight the critical conceptual relationships that organize the formation of young people as workers. My analysis is focused on the productive aspects of the self, the practices that cultivate these aspects and the relationship between labour and value that makes up young people's identities as workers. These are the key issues at stake in the creation of young people as subjects of value to the labour force. By attention to these issues, my method positions young people as critical to the post-Fordist work ethic, itself understood as a conceptual formation designed to provide insight into the relationship between youth, labour and value in post-Fordist capitalism.

References

Abrahams, J. 2017. Honourable Mobility or Shameless Entitlement? Habitus and Graduate Employment. *British Journal of Sociology of Education*, 38(5), 625–640.

Adkins, L. 2002. *Revisions: Gender and Sexuality in Late Modernity*, Buckingham: Open University Press.

Adkins, L. 2005a. Social Capital: The Anatomy of a Troubled Concept. *Feminist Theory*, 6(2), 195–211.

Adkins, L. 2005b. The New Economy, Property and Personhood. *Theory, Culture and Society*, 22(1), 111–130.

Adkins, L. 2017. Disobedient Workers, the Law and the Making of Unemployment Markets. *Sociology*, 51(2), 290–305.

Adkins, L. & Lury, C. 1999. The Labour of Identity: Performing Identities, Performing Economies. *Economy and Society*, 28(4), 598–614.

Adkins, L. & Dever, M. 2016. *The Post-Fordist Sexual Contract: Working and Living in Contingency*, Basingstoke: Palgrave.

Allen, K. & Hollingworth, S. 2013. 'Sticky Subjects' or 'Cosmopolitan Creatives'? Social Class, Place and Urban Young People's Aspirations for Work in the Knowledge Economy. *Urban Studies*, 50(3), 499–517.

Amin, A. (ed.) 2003. *Post-Fordism: A Reader*, Oxford: Blackwell.

Andres, L. & Wyn, J. 2010. *The Making of a Generation: The Children of the 1970s in Adulthood*, Toronto, Buffalo: University of Toronto Press.

Ball, S. 1993. Education Markets, Choice and Social Class: The Market as a Class Strategy in the UK and the USA. *British Journal of Sociology of Education*, 14(1), 3–19.

Ball, S. 2006. The Necessity and Violence of Social Theory. *Discourse: Studies in the Cultural Politics of Education*, 27(1), 3–10.

Ball, S., Maguire, M. & Macrae, S. 2000. Space, Work and the 'New Urban Economies'. *Journal of Youth Studies*, 3(3), 279–300.

Banet-Weiser, S. 2012. *Authentic TM: The Politics of Ambivalence in a Brand Culture*, New York, London: New York University Press.

Bauman, Z. 2000. *Liquid Modernity*, Cambridge: Polity Press.

Beck, U. 1992. *Risk Society. Towards a New Modernity*, London: Sage.

Beck, U. 2000. *The Brave New World of Work*, Malden, MA: Blackwell.

Besen-Cassino, Y. 2014. *Consuming Work: Youth Labour in America*, Philadelphia, PA: Temple University Press.

Bolton, S. 2009. The Lady Vanishes: Women's Work and Affective Labour. *International Journal of Work Organisation and Emotion*, 3(1), 72–80.

Bourdieu, P. 1984. *Distinction: A Social Critique of the Judgement of Taste*, Cambridge, MA: Harvard University Press.

Bourdieu, P. 1990. *The Logic of Practice*, Cambridge: Polity.

Brannen, J. & Nilsen, J. 2005. Individualisation, Choice and Structure: A Discussion of Current Trends in Sociological Analysis. *The Sociological Review*, 53(3), 412–428.

BSL. 2014. *Australian Youth Unemployment: Snapshot*, Fitzroy: Brotherhood of St Laurence.

Burke, C. 2016. *Culture, Capitals and Graduate Futures: Degrees of Class*, London: Routledge.

Burke, C., Scurry, T. & Blenkinsopp, J. 2019. Navigating the Graduate Labour Market: The Impact of Social Class on Student Understandings of Graduate Careers and the Graduate Labour Market. *Studies in Higher Education*, 45(2), 1711–1722.

Carson, E., Winefield, A. H., Waters, L. & Kerr, L. 2003. Work for the Dole: A Pathway to Self-Esteem and Employment Commitment, or Road to Frustration? *Youth Studies Australia*, 22(4), 19–26.

Chesters, J., Smith, J., Cuervo, H., Laughland-Booy, J., Wyn, J., Skrbis, Z. & Woodman, D. 2018. Young Adulthood in Uncertain Times: The Association between Sense of Personal Control and Employment, Education, Personal Relationships and Health. *Journal of Sociology*, 55(2), 389–408.

Cote, J. 2014. Towards a New Political Economy of Youth. *Journal of Youth Studies*, 17(4), 527–543.

Cote, J. 2016. A New Political Economy of Youth Reprised: Rejoinder to France and Threadgold. *Journal of Youth Studies*, 19(6), 852–868.

Cuzzocrea, V. 2015. Young People and Employability. In: Wyn, J. (ed) *Handbook of Childhood and Youth Studies*, Singapore: Springer, 557–568.

Farrugia, D. 2013a. The Reflexive Subject: Towards a Theory of Reflexivity as Practical Intelligibility. *Current Sociology*, 61(3), 283–300.

Farrugia, D. 2013b. Young People and Structural Inequality: Beyond the Middle Ground. *Journal of Youth Studies*, 16(5), 679–693.

Farrugia, D. 2018a. *Spaces of Youth: Work, Citizenship and Culture in a Global Context*, Abingdon, New York: Routledge.

Farrugia, D. 2018b. Youthfulness and Immaterial Labour in the New Economy. *The Sociological Review*, 66(3), 511–526.

Farrugia, D. 2019. Class, Place and Mobility beyond the Global City: Stigmatisation and the Cosmopolitanisation of the Local. *Journal of Youth Studies*, 23(2), 237–251.

Farrugia, D. 2020. Youth, Work and Global Capitalism: New Directions. *Journal of Youth Studies*, https://doi.org/10.1080/13676261.2020.1729 965.

Foucault, M. 1988. Technologies of the Self. In: Martin, L.H., Gutman, H. & Hutton, P.H. (eds) *Technologies of the Self: A Seminar with Michel Foucault*, Amherst: University of Massachusetts Press.

Foucault, M. 2004. *The Birth of Biopolitics*, Basingstoke: Palgrave Macmillan.

France, A. & Threadgold, S. 2016. Youth and Political Economy: Towards a Bourdieusian Approach. *Journal of Youth Studies*, 19(5), 612–628.

France, A., Roberts, S. & Wood, B. 2018. Youth, Social Class and Privilege in the Antipodes: Towards a New Research Agenda for Youth Sociology. *Journal of Sociology*, 54(3), 362–380.

Friedli, L. & Stearn, R. 2015. Positive Affect as Coercive Strategy: Conditionality, Activation and the Role of Psychology in UK Government Workfare Programmes. *Critical Medical Humanities*, 41(1), 40–47.

Furlong, A. & Cartmel, F. 2007. *Young People and Social Change: New Perspectives*, Maidenhead: McGraw Hill/Open University Press.

Furlong, A., Goodwin, J., O'Connor, H., Hadfield, S., Hall, S., Lowden, K. & Plugor, R. 2017. *Young People in the Labour Market: Past, Present, Future*, Abingdon, New York: Routledge.

Gerrard, J. 2014. All that is Solid Melts into Work: Self-Work, the 'Learning Ethic' and the Work Ethic. *The Sociological Review*, 62(4), 862–879.

Gill, R. & Pratt, A. 2008. In the Social Factory? Immaterial Labour, Precariousness and Cultural Work. *Theory, Culture and Society*, 25 (7–8), 1–30.

Griffin, C. 1993. *Representations of Youth: The Study of Youth and Adolescence in Britain and America*, Cambridge: Polity Press.

Haikkola, L. 2019. Shaping Activation Policy at the Street Level: Governing Inactivity in Youth Employment Services. *Acta Sociologica*, 62(3), 334–348.

Hardt, M. & Negri, A. 2004. *Multitude*, New York: Penguin Press.

Jarrett, K. 2015. *Feminism, Labour and Digital Media: The Digital Housewife*, London, New York: Routledge.

Kelly, P. 2006. The Entrepreneurial Self and 'Youth at Risk': Exploring the Horizons of Identity in the 21st Century. *Journal of Youth Studies*, 9(1), 17–32.

Kelly, P. & Harrison, L. 2009. *Working in Jamie's Kitchen: Salvation, Passion and Young Workers*, New York: Palgrave.

Kenway, J., Kraack, A. & Hickey-Moodey, A. 2006. *Masculinity Beyond the Metropolis*, Houndmills, Basingstoke: Palgrave Macmillan.

Lamont, M. 2000. *The Dignity of Working Men*, New York: Russell Sage Foundation.

Law, J. 2004. *After Method*, London, New York: Routledge.

Lawler, S. 2005. Disgusted Subjects: The Making of Middle-Class Identities. *The Sociological Review*, 53(3), 429–446.

Lazzarato, M. 1996. Immaterial Labour. In: Virno, P. & Hardt, M. (eds) *Radical Thought in Italy: A Potential Politics*, Minneapolis, London: University of Minnesota Press, 133–150.

Loveday, V. 2015. Working-Class Participation, Middle-Class Aspiration? Value, Upward Mobility and Symbolic Indebtedness in Higher Education. *The Sociological Review*, 63(3), 570–588.

MacDonald, R. 2011. Youth Transitions, Unemployment and Underemployment. *Journal of Sociology*, 47(4), 427–444.

MacDonald, R., Mason, P. & Shildrick, T. 2001. Snakes & ladders: In Defence of Studies of Youth Transition. *Sociological Research Online*, 5(4), 1–13.

Marx, K. (1978) 'Estranged Labour'. In Tucker, R. C. (ed.) *The Marx-Engels Reader*, Second Edition, New York & London: W. W. Norton.

McDowell, L. 2003. *Redundant Masculinities? Employment Change and White Working Class Youth*, Malden: Blackwell.

McRobbie, A. 2011. Reflections on Feminism, Immaterial Labour and the Post-Fordist Regime. *New Formations*, 70, 60–76.

McRobbie, A. 2016. *Be Creative*, Cambridge: Polity.

Mizen, P. 2004. *The Changing State of Youth*, Houndmills: Palgrave Macmillan.

Nayak, A. 2006. Displaced Masculinities: Chavs, Youth and Class in the Post-Industrial City. *Sociology*, 40(5), 813–831.

Nolan, B. & Whelan, C. T. 1996. *Resources, Deprivation and Poverty*, Oxford: Clarendon Press.

Peck, J. & Tickell, A. 2002. Neoliberalising Space. In: Brenner, N. & Theodore, N. (eds) *Spaces of Neoliberalism: Urban Restructuring in North America and Western Europe*, Oxford: Blackwell, 33–57.

Reay, D. 2005. Beyond Consciousness? The Psychic Landscape of Social Class. *Sociology*, 39(5), 911–928.

Roberts, S. 2012. One Step Forward, One Step Beck: A Contribution to the Ongoing Conceptual Debate in Youth Studies. *Journal of Youth Studies*, 15(3), 389–401.

Roberts, S. 2018. *Working-Class Men in Transition*, New York: Routledge.

Rose, N. 1999. *Governing the Soul*, London: Free Association Books.

Rosenberg, M. 2015. The Conceptual Articulation of the Reality of Life: Max Weber's Theoretical Constitution of Sociological Ideal Types. *Journal of Classical Sociology*, 16(1), 84–101.

Savage, M. 2003. A New Class Paradigm? *British Journal of Sociology of Education*, 24(4), 535–541.

Savage, M., Devine, F., Cunningham, N., Taylor, M., Li, Y., Hjellbrekke, J., Le Roux, B., Friedman, S. & Miles, A. 2013. A New Model of Social Class? Findings from the BBC's Great British Class Survey Experiment. *Sociology*, 47(2), 219–250.

Sayer, A. 2005. *The Moral Significance of Class*, Cambridge: Cambridge University Press.

Sennett, R. & Cobb, J. 1972. *The Hidden Injuries of Class*, Cambridge: Cambridge University Press.

Shamir, B. 1986. Self-Esteem and the Psychological Impact of Unemployment. *Social Psychology Quarterly*, 49(1), 61–72.

Sheppard, E. & Leitner, H. 2010. Quo Vadis Neoliberalism? The Remaking of Global Capitalist Governance After the Washington Consensus. *Geoforum*, 41(2), 185–194.

Simmons, R., Thompson, R. & Russell, L. 2014. *Education, Work and Social Change: Young People and Marginalisation in Post-Industrial Britain*, Basingstoke: Palgrave Macmillan.

Skeggs, B. 1997. *Formations of Class and Gender: Becoming Respectable*, London, Thousand Oaks, CA: Sage.

Skeggs, B. 2004. *Class, Self, Culture*, London: Routledge.

Skeggs, B. 2005. The Making of Class and Gender through Visualising Moral Subject Formation. *Sociology*, 39(5), 965–982.

Skeggs, B. 2011. Imagining Personhood Differently: Person Value and Autonomist Working-Class Value Practices. *The Sociological Review*, 59(3), 496–513.

Strangleman, T. 2012. Work Identity in Crisis? Rethinking the Problem of Attachment and Loss at Work. *Sociology*, 46(3), 411–425.

Strangleman, T. 2015. Rethinking Industrial Citizenship: The Role and Meaning of Work in an Age of Austerity. *The British Journal of Sociology*, 66(4), 673–690.

Sukarieh, M. & Tannock, S. 2008. In the Best Interests of Youth or Neoliberalism? The World Bank and the New Global Youth Emplowerment Project. *Journal of Youth Studies*, 11(3), 301–312.

Sukarieh, M. & Tannock, S. 2014. *Youth Rising?*, London: Routledge.

Sukarieh, M. & Tannock, S. 2016. On the Political Economy of Youth: A Comment. *Journal of Youth Studies*, 19, 1281–1289.

Tannock, S. 2001. *Youth at Work: The Unionised Fast Food and Grocery Workplace*, Philadelphia, PA: Temple University Press.

Thompson, E. P. 1980. *The Making of the English Working Class*, New York: Pantheon.

Threadgold, S. & Nilan, P. 2009. Reflexivity of Contemporary Youth, Risk, and Cultural Capital. *Current Sociology*, 57(1), 47–68.

Threadgold, S. 2011. Should I Pitch my Tent in the Middle Ground? On 'Middling Tendency', Beck and Inequality in Youth Sociology. *Journal of Youth Studies*, 14(4), 381–393.

Threadgold, S. 2018. *Youth, Class and Everyday Struggles*, London: Routledge.

Turner, B. 2001. The Erosion of Citizenship. *British Journal of Sociology*, 52(2), 189–209.

Tyler, I. 2013. *Revolting Subjects: Social Abjection and Resistance in Neoliberal Britain*, London: Zed Books.

Tyler, I. 2015. Classificatory Struggles: Class, Culture and Inequality in Neoliberal Times. *The Sociological Review*, 63(2), 493–511.

Weber, M. 1949. 'Objectivity' in Social Science and Social Policy. In: Shils, E. & Finch, H. (eds) *Max Weber on The Methodology of the Social Sciences*, Glencoe, IL: The Free Press of Glencoe, 50–112.

Weber, M., Owen, D. & Strong, T. 2004. *The Vocation Lectures*, Indianapolis, IN, Cambridge: Hackett Publishing Company.

Weeks, K. 2011. *The Problem with Work*, Durham, NC, London: Duke University Press.

Willis, P. 1977. *Learning to Labour: How Working Class Kids Get Working Class Jobs*, Farnborough: Saxon House.

Woodman, D. 2009. The Mysterious Case of the Pervasive Choice Biography: Ulrich Beck, Structure/Agency, and the Middling State of Theory in the Sociology of Youth. *Journal of Youth Studies*, 12(3), 243–256.

Woodman, D. & Wyn, J. 2015. *Youth and Generation: Rethinking Change and Inequality in the Lives of Young People*, Los Angeles, London, Washington DC, Delhi, Singapore: Sage.

World Bank. 2007. *World Development Report: Development and the Next Generation*, Washington DC: The International Bank for Reconstruction and Development.

Wyn, J. & White, R. 1997. *Rethinking Youth*, St Leonards: Allen and Unwin.

Yoon, K. 2014. Transnational Youth Mobility in the Neoliberal Economy of Experience. *Journal of Youth Studies*, 17(8), 1014–1028.

Index